Queen Elizabeth 2

CONTENTS

QUEEN ELIZABETH 2
FAREWELL SEASON 2008

FOREWORD

QE2 BRITAIN WAVES GOODBYE.

QE2 was conceived and developed in Liverpool within the solid walls of the magnificent Cunard Building on the Pier Head so it is true to say that this great city and the most famous ship in the world have a very close bond. And, it was most fitting that QE2 was the ship chosen to be alongside at the opening of the Liverpool Cruise Facility by HRH The Duke of Kent last September.

QE2's call to the city on Friday 3 October will not only be her ninth at the port but also her final as in November this year QE2 will leave Cunard service and head for another great port city, Dubai, where she will start a new life as a first-class hotel and exhibition centre.

QE2's record has no equal. In almost 40 years of Cunard service she has sailed over 5.8 million nautical miles, more than any ship ever; carried over 2.5 million guests on over 800 transatlantic crossings and 25 World Cruises; been commanded by 25 Captains and dashed to the Falkland Islands when her country needed her in 1982. She is still the fastest passenger ship in the world and undoubtedly the most beautiful!

The Cunard lion, of course, continues to roar with Queen Mary 2 and Queen Victoria carrying on the Cunard traditions set down by over 200 ships during the company's 168-year history and maintained by QE2 alone for so long. However, the Cunard fleet will not be without an 'Elizabeth' in the fleet for long, as the new Queen Elizabeth enters service in 2010.

QE2's welcome when she has visited Liverpool has been legendary and I'm sure this final call will be no exception. And, we look forward to Tuesday 20 October 2009 when our flagship Queen Mary 2 makes her maiden call into Liverpool, our ancestral home, during her fifth anniversary year. Queen Mary 2 will be the largest vessel of any kind to sail up the Mersey and I can't wait to see her alongside the Landing Stage – what a spectacular sight that will be!

But for now let's celebrate QE2's final visit. I look forward to it greatly.

Carol Marlow

President and Managing Director. Cunard

INTRODUCTION

IN HER 41 YEARS IN SERVICE, Cunard Line's Queen Elizabeth 2 has claimed countless records and notable achievements.

It's unlikely we will ever see such records set again.

That fact - perhaps more than any of her other amazing accolades - mark out QE2's place in British maritime history.

Last year, during her 40th anniversary lap of honour around Britain tens of thousands of people turned out around the coast and at her ports of call

These well-wishers ranged in age from retired Clydeside shipyard workers whose skills had helped create QE2, to the grand children of early crew members.

They represented a variety of wide-ranging links to the ship, but shared a common pride in being able to stake their own personal claim to an association with the most famous ocean liner in the world.

It has again been a pleasure to meet some of these people, to trigger their memories and record their recollections of QE2.

For them, and everyone else around the world with long and fond memories of this great Liner, it will soon be time to wave goodbye. This time saddened by the knowledge she will not sail our way again.

TONY STOREY
Liverpool
August 2008

Slipway to Sunset

❖ In the 41 years since her launch in 1967, Queen Elizabeth 2 has become the most famous ship in the world.

She has captured headlines and countless imaginations all over the globe - a globe whose oceans have carried her almost 6 million nautical miles from construction on the Clyde to retirement in Dubai.

There has simply never been another ship quite like the QE2.

Her creation itself amounted to a minor miracle.

❖ FUNDING FOR THE PROJECT proved difficult to secure. In the swinging sixties there were plenty of potential backers ready to believe the age of ocean travel was a thing of the past.

With the jet-engined Comet able to fly from London to New York in a matter of hours, what was the point of taking five or six days about it?

When Cunard Line's owners did eventually reach agreement with the government over support for the ship to replace the veteran liners Queen Elizabeth and Queen Mary, the country's industrial relations were not at their best.

QE2 was brought to life on the banks of the Upper Clyde. But it was by no means an easy birth.

When, eventually, Her Majesty Queen Elizabeth II, stepped towards the microphone on the Royal Platform above the slipway at John Brown's shipyard on September, 20, 1967, uncertainty still abounded.

Not least over the name the young Queen was about to bestow upon the huge hull of steel sitting in front of her and towering over the guests.

In the weeks before the launch day, speculation about its name was rife. At that stage the ship was known only as order number 736.

In the traditions of the launching ceremony, the Queen was handed an envelope containing a slip of paper on which the proposed name of the new liner had been written.

A written reminder of the ship's name was considered essential after one VIP reportedly forgot the name of the vessel over which they had been invited to officiate.

A similar envelope to the one on the Clydebank

launch platform was resting in the safe at Cunard's New York office in case of some slip up on this side of the Atlantic.

The Queen declined the envelope, reportedly joking: 'I won't be needing that'. Seconds later, at the microphone and speaking in a clear and confident voice, Her Majesty said: 'I name this ship Queen Elizabeth the Second. May God bless her and all who sail in her.'

The Queen then used a pair of gold scissors to cut a ribbon releasing a bottle of Australian white wine against the hull of the liner. These were the same scissors that her mother and grandmother had previously used at ceremonies to launch their namesake vessels.

The envelope that she had declined to accept had contained the name Queen Elizabeth.

THE QUEEN AND DUKE OF EDINBURGH WITH SHIPYARD DIRECTOR GEORGE PARKER DURING THE LAUNCH.

❖AFTER THE LAUNCH Cunard's then Chairman Sir Basil Smallpiece consulted with royal aides and it was agreed that the suffix 'Second' would be written as the Arabic '2'and not the Roman 'II'.

This was considered a sensible move for a variety of reasons. At the time only battleships had carried a reigning monarch's Roman numeral suffix, and the Queen was, in fact only Queen Elizabeth I of Scotland – thus to name the ship with 'II' could have offended the people of the country which had produced the hull of the new liner and, critically for Cunard, who were still required to fit her out for service.

Forty one years on, *Queen Elizabeth 2* has become the most famous ship in the world as well as the one whose name is so often misprinted.

❖ NOW SHE IS APPROACHING RETIREMENT By the time she arrives in her final port of call at Dubai she will have completed 1,428 voyages, clocking up 5.9 million nautical miles and having carried almost 2.5m passengers from pop stars and preachers to prime ministers and presidents.

She will have crossed the ocean she could call her home in the hostile North Atlantic- 806 times, calling at New York 710 times.

Her home port of Southampton will have welcomed her and waved her off 730 times on 25 occasions to embark on full world cruises.

It's unlikely that her record of achievements will ever be matched or beaten.

Put simply, there is only one QE2!

The most famous ship in the world has earned her place in the sun.

Captain Ian McNaught's Farewell

❖ AFTER SPENDING 22 YEARS of his career at sea on board QE2 Captain Ian McNaught is preparing himself for an emotional farewell to the liner he calls his second home.

He will be in command for QE2's final voyage form Southampton to Dubai.

He is however, convinced the time is right for the ship to sail into retirement – and that her new owners appreciate the icon they have bought.

He says: "We've got to get our heads round this and accept that come November that's it. And it is right and proper that it goes now when it's still good at what it does and is still very much respected. I would hate to see it be stretched out another ten years and become a little bit tired and a little but worn and not so good any more, so the time is right."

The Captain's immense pride in his command is evident.

"For me, there will never be another one of these." He speaks with a passion about his 41 year old ship.

"There is only one QE2. It's the last great British liner. It's this icon of the sixties, and you look at her and you think of Concorde, which has gone now of course, sadly. The Queen when she launched it was a very young Queen. And I think this and Concorde and the Beatles and all that sort of thing stood for an awful lot in the sixties and here we are - some forty years later we've reached the end of its life."

"It will be emotional. We all will be. My wife's coming on that voyage and she says it's just to bring the Kleenex! It will be sad, never to be coming back. It will be very sad," says the Captain.

QE2 has welcomed a significant number of first time guests since the announcement of her sale.

"It's amazing how many first time passengers have been on saying 'Oh we thought we'd better come on board because we missed Concorde so we thought we'd better come on QE2 instead'. They want to get it before it goes and they know they will never have the chance again. And they have been on modern cruise ships, but they wanted to come on here before it finishes just to see what it's like. And many of them are surprised and they say: 'We didn't expect it to be like this. It's friendly and happy and it's not starchy. It's formal and we like the getting dressed up thing, but it's so friendly on here, not like the modern ships'. And that's great. QE2 really is an icon isn't it?"

Since the day she launched the ship on the Clyde in 1967, Her Majesty the Queen has taken particular interest in the longest serving Cunarder.

❖ THE ROYAL FAREWELL last June was another remarkable day for the ship, its Captain and his crew.

"The Queen came to see us on 2nd June," recalls Captain McNaught.

"That was a massive day for everybody in the ship and it was so great because the theme of the visit was for her to meet as many of the crew as possible. And I think she really enjoyed the day. And certainly the crew enjoyed having her on board. She was here for just over three hours and she very kindly went through the Embarkation Hall in the terminal so she could be seen by some of the embarking passengers in the afternoon, so she really did see as many people as she possibly could."

He adds: "It was a big day for QE2, To have the Queen come down, just to see the ship and just to see us, was a highlight of my career on QE2. A terrific honour and I really do think she enjoyed the visit.

"We talked a lot about Britannia (the former Royal Yacht) at the lunch table and what Britannia meant for her and compared that to what this ship means to us, and I think she has a lot of respect for this ship."

The Royal Visit came as QE2 and her crew prepared for her final season of departures from her home port of Southampton.

Captain McNaught knows the final departure in November looms large for many of his crew.

"I think the saddest bit of all will be when we go out of Southampton. The voyage itself, I hope, will become a two and a half week long party and celebration of what's gone on and everybody just gets on with the business of enjoying the ship."

"AND I THINK DUBAI, that's going to be quite a big celebration as the ship gets in. But I think when we actually let go and blow that whistle and start heading out of Southampton for the last time, I think that'll be tough. That will be hard. Never coming back."

There is a curiosity – some may say anxiety – among many devoted QE2 fans to know what is gong to happen to the ship in Dubai when she is converted into a destination attraction.

"Guests want to know what's going to happen to her in Dubai," says the Captain.

"They are really interested. Many have said they wont come on the last voyage because they know they just could not cope with the emotion of it all. There is a general sadness about it all but I think at the same time there is quite a lot of pleasure in the fact that she is not just going to disappear and go to scrap or be sold on to some not so great owner who just wants to run her as a cheap ferry somewhere, or just run her into the ground for every penny he can get.

"I think there is a lot of pleasure in the fact that after this big refit in Dubai she will be a hotel but it will still be the QE2 and that is important to people. I think, that if they do go and visit the ship, once they step inside it will be 'Wow it's the QE2' and not just a hotel in a metal box.'

Captain McNaught believes QE2's new owners have the financial resources to ensure the ship has a long and spectacular retirement and doubts a similar future could be assured in Britain.

How QE2 could look in Dubai

"I know a lot of people say it's such a shame she is not going to stay in the UK but you have to think of the practicalities and if you look at Britannia it takes an awful lot of £7.50's or whatever it is to maintain a ship, so we have to be honest about this and ask: 'Who's got the wherewithal in the UK to look after this, maintain it. Where do you put it?"

"So I think she's going in the right place and what's so good about Dubai is what she has to compete with is very, very high standard, so to make it work, this has to be a very high standard as well. There is going to be a lot of money lavished on her so when she does come back to her berth after this period of just over a year she is going to be top class.

"Dubai have brought her because of what she is and what she means to people – the history and that little bit of class that she can bring to Dubai because yes, they have the most wonderful hotels in the world but there is not a class act there yet – there's no Ritz, there's no big names there. This is going to be the big name. That's a good dignified retirement for the ship."

Like many of his ship's company, Captain McNaught is preparing himself for the final voyage with mixed emotions.

"This isn't just a place of work, it's a second home for us all, and I am a new boy I've only been here 22 years," he jokes.

"There is a very tight relationship for us as a ship's company so when the big day comes and we all get split, sent around the rest of the fleet, that'll be tough on a lot of people. There's a lot of good friends on here, long time friends, but to leave this behind when we finally take the Cunard house flag down and put the Dubai one up, and then shut her down for them, that'll be hard.

"Yes, it'll be hard for people. They will miss it. But, there is an awful lot in here that can ever be taken away. For crew and guests, the memories will be cherished.

"When we do finally put it in the dry dock and we start shutting the ship down for them, the ship does die really doesn't it?

"And once they start taking bits and pieces out of it, we know that the man engine plant is coming out – we don't want to be here to see that. We'll take it in and park it for them and turn it all off and then I think we need to go because I think it would be just too upsetting to watch it all get pulled apart."

The Captain hopes to return when the 'pulling apart' is complete.

"Hopefully in a year or so we'll see it in its new guise. I think that will be really interesting. I would love to do that because I would like to see what they have done with it. There are a lot of areas in the ship which will stay as they are now but it will be interesting to see what they do because the ship has to change. It's changing function so it does have to change to a certain extent and it would be nice to see what they have done.

"When you look at it, it's still got to shout QE2. That's what they are buying. You've got to be able to look at it and recognise it and that's important as well."

❖ TWO DAYS ABOVE ALL OTHERS STAND OUT IN THE CAPTAIN'S MEMORY OF LIFE ON BOARD QE2.

"The two big days are the first day you ever come here – not knowing what to expect. You have no real idea of what's going to be here – and it's the QE2.

"And then I suppose the next biggest day is your very first day as Captain. That's the other big day really for me. You're supposed to know everything – of course you don't know everything – not by a long chalk – but you have to look as though you know everything, so they are the two big days.

"On that first day as Captain we were bound for New York. It was a good way to start. and I remember I got three days into the crossing and my wife sent me an email saying: 'Oh well, you've got further than Captain Smith did on the Titanic.' That was a great confidence booster!"

Among many other highlights for Captain McNaught was last year's 40th birthday lap of honour around the UK – with calls in his native Tyneside and at Cunard Line's spiritual home in Liverpool most memorable.

"Getting into Newcastle, taking this ship in there for the very first time, was a big, big thing for me despite being late because of the bad weather but we got there.

"Everywhere we went that week the ship was applauded and there was a fantastic atmosphere inside the ship but also on the shore as well. I think for those people that were new to the QE2, both in the management side and in the passenger side, I think they were just completely overwhelmed by what happened. Forty years down the line and people still come out in their thousands."

Low cloud and torrential rain marred the dawn arrival in Liverpool where QE2's call was to mark the official opening of the city's new cruise liner terminal and guests were to attend a celebration concert at one of the city's Cathedrals.

"It was a bit wet, but you know we all went into that Cathedral and when we came out the sun was shining and the sky was blue. Sun shone on the righteous!

"It was a big, big day and so good for us to be able to go alongside there instead of sitting in the river. That makes a huge difference. It's really going to open up the port for passenger liners and cruise ships.

"The call suddenly becomes attractive. When you come in there and you have the three buildings there, the Three Graces it's magnificent.

"I now when Grand Princess goes to Liverpool, it's still an impressive big white ship but it does not have the heart that this one has and I think that's what people come out to look at - what this thing stands for. It's tremendous. Everyone associated with this year's round Britain farewell expects even bigger crowds in ports of call around the UK and Ireland. Everybody knows that this time is the last time so I think there will be a lot of people out to see QE2 and it makes us feel very special. It really does. It's great," explains the Captain.

"I think there will be some big crowds - because it is the last one and the timings for some of the ports are more flexible to people coming to see us.

"And it's the end of an era, but come five years time – I hope – Queen Mary 2 and Queen Victoria and the new Queen Elizabeth become the standards to be set for everybody."

❖I HOPE THAT THE TIMES WILL ALLOW A LOT MORE PEOPLE TO ENJOY COMING TO SEE US COME IN OR GO OUT – ONE OF THE TWO - AND IT IS THE LAST TIME. I THINK THAT WILL BRING ONE OR TWO MORE PEOPLE OUT."

Captain McNaught believes QE2's sister ships, the mighty Queen Mary 2 and the stylish Queen Victoria, will earn their place in the affection of passengers.

"I know QM2 is going to Liverpool, and the sheer scale of the thing is so impressive, but until we have gone, I don't think people have a heart for it yet, like they have for QE2.

"When the old Queen Mary and the Queen Elizabeth went, and this thing arrived everybody said it's the end of the world – this big, ugly 1960's designed thing – oh it's horrible.

"But give it a few years and this has become the classic .And I think the same will happen again. When this one goes there'll be, well, not quite a period of mourning, but people will say isn't it sad it's gone?

"And it's the end of an era, but come five years time – I hope – Queen Mary 2 and Queen Victoria and the new Queen Elizabeth become the standards to be set for everybody."

Despite his hope for the future, Captain McNaught knows as well as anyone who has ever served or travelled on board QE2 that there will never be another like her.

"For me, there will never be another one of these. This is it. You can't get any higher than this. I think this just means so much to people and to be part of this is very special. For me this is it. This is something I grew up looking at as a boy thinking: 'That's the one!', And here we are."

REFLECTIONS OF COMMODORE WARWICK

❖ A MORSE CODE MESSAGE FLASHED TO A CARGO SHIP WAS TO SPARK A LIFELONG INTEREST IN QE2 FOR LIVERPOOL-BORN CUNARD LINE COMMODORE RON WARWICK.

He was serving as Second Mate on the cargo vessel Jamaica Producer in the mid-1960s when his father, Commodore William E Warwick, was appointed as the QE2's first Master Designate.

"The Radio Officer told me he had read about the appointment when he received the daily news by Morse code. On my return to London, I collected all the press cuttings about my father, and subsequently became interested in the ship itself. Ever since, and up to the present day, I have kept and filed press cuttings and articles about the QE2", recalls the retired Commodore.

The cuttings in his unique collection chart the remarkable history of the ship his father brought into service and he took command of in 1990. A huge part of QE2's successful 41 year history spans separate periods when the father and son were in command of the vessel.

I was so impressed by the ship that I decided the only way to go to sea was on a liner.
A few months later I applied for a position with Cunard Line and joined the company in April 1970 with the goal, and a lot of hope, of being the Captain of QE2 one day

Commodore Ron Warwick recalls the time he first saw the QE2 – during sea trials in the English Channel.

"I first saw the QE2 when she was carrying out some trials in the English Channel. I was outward bound from London on another ship and our Radio Officer heard the QE2 working Portishead (by Morse Code in those days) so he sent a message to the ship for me. An hour or so later the QE2 came up on our stern and passed us a mile or so off at full speed. It was a very impressive sight."

The Commodore's first visit to his father's Command was in Kingston, Jamaica.

"I went on board Queen Elizabeth 2 for the first time when she was on her inaugural winter cruise season and called at Kingston. At that time I was also in port on my ship."

"Compared to my 18 year old, 6159 gt cargo ship, she was a palace and I remember being quite overwhelmed by the technology on the bridge and the magnificence of the interior décor. I particularly remember the Captain's quarters and saying to my father that I had no idea he lived in such luxury."

He added: "I was so impressed by the ship that I decided the only way to go to sea was on a liner. A few months later I applied for a position with Cunard Line and joined the company in April 1970 with the goal, and a lot of hope, of being the Captain of QE2 one day."

His ambitions were exceeded one wet and miserable day in Southampton in January 2004.

"When the original Queen Mary and Queen Elizabeth left the Fleet, the appointment of Commodore ceased to be made as a matter of course. Accordingly, it was never held by the senior Captain of the day. By the late 1990s the position appeared to have been phased out so it was a great and most unexpected honour to receive the appointment from Carnival Corporation & plc CEO Micky Arison and Cunard Line President Pam Conover on the day Queen Mary 2 arrived in Southampton for the first time." explains the Commodore.

His promotion to 'Commodare' completed another unique chapter in the history of the sea-faring Warwick family and the Line served by father and son.

❖COMMODORE WARWICK REMEMBERS some of his father's early associations with QE2 overseeing her final construction and fitting out at the John Brown shipyard on the Clyde.

"I was away a lot of the time and did not get to see my father much during the building. However, from time to time we met up and he would tell me what he had been up too. He had offices in Lower Regent Street, London, at South Western House in Southampton and a flat in Scotland so he was always on the move. He spent a lot of time investigating navigation equipment and visited the major manufacturers of the day. He sailed on cross channel ferries to assess different types of radars. Once I remember him saying he had been trying out chairs all day to approve the suitability of them being used on board in inclement weather."

Throughout its construction QE2 was known only as Order Number 736 – the title designated by the John Brown yard.

Speculation – and suggestions – about what the magnificent new liner should be christened was never in short supply.

"My father's secretary in the London office had the task of dealing with the hundreds of letters written to Cunard with suggestions for the name of the ship. I still have a bundle of the letters which I found in his study after he passed away but I have yet to look through them," explains the Commodore.

His collection of QE2 memorabilia does not include an invitation to the ship launch by HM the Queen.

Commodore Warwick explains: "My father asked me if I would like to attend the launching but unfortunately I was going to be away at sea so could not attend. Many years later I wished I had accepted and then declined so at least I would have had the invitation as a souvenir!"

For a significant part of the ship's history the Warwick family has made a major contribution to its success, enjoying dozens of memorable experiences along the way.

The memories are so vast and vivid that Commodore Warwick says it is hard to single any out.

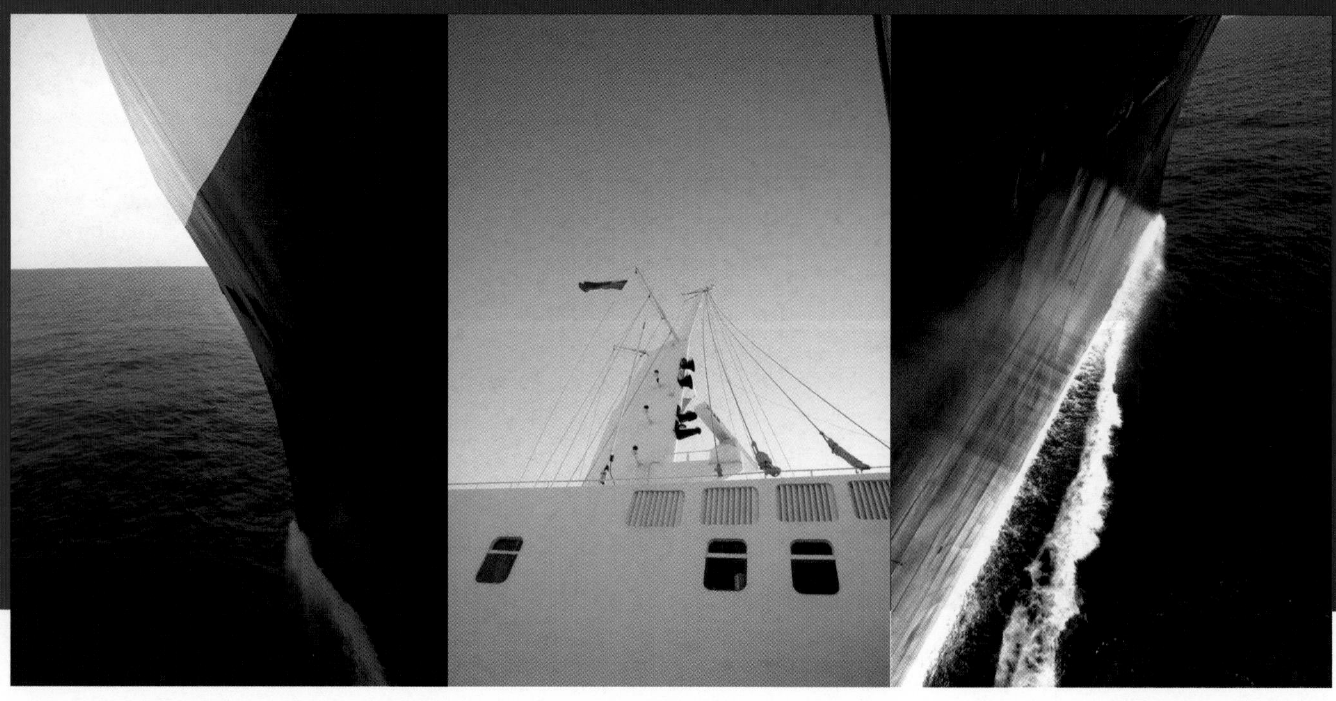

"There have been so many memorable experiences that it is hard to single out one that has been better than the others," he explains.

"Transiting the Panama Canal for the first time (in 1975) was very impressive. Thousands of spectators came out to see these two elements of man made grandeur link together. During my career I transited the Canal 50 times and I never tired of the experience.

"From the Bridge I witnessed bomb disposal expert's parachute into the mid Atlantic in appalling weather conditions to deal with a bomb threat. I witnessed lots of un-cruise like activity when we sailed with troops to the Falklands; attended distressed seafarers and participated in numerous helicopter evacuations.

"I have shown many dignitaries around the Bridge and perhaps most significantly, welcomed HM The Queen on the Bridge during Cunard's 150th anniversary in 1990."

QE2's iconic status – and in particular her place in British maritime history comes as no surprise to the Commodore.

"At heart, the UK is a maritime nation but in this day and age we have little to remind us of it. Seeing the QE2 awakes the memories and reminds us of when the country was a world leader in all aspects of the shipping industry," reflects the Commodore.

The QE2's 40th Anniversary tour of Britain round he British Isles gave the retired Commodore the opportunity to enjoy all the ship had to offer.

"I was a passenger and as such really enjoyed experiencing the ship from a different perspective. I liked the freedom of not having to watch the clock (except for meal time!) and having the time to talk to others for as long as I wished and to wonder around observing the ship from different positions whilst docking rather than just being on the Bridge. It was a memorable week."

❖ AMONG THE HIGHLIGHTS OF THE TOUR WAS QE2'S RETURN TO CUNARD LINE'S SPIRITUAL HOME LIVERPOOL.

"I think the people of Liverpool have always regarded the QE2 as 'their' ship and all the welcomes have been consistently warm and welcoming. Last September was no exception."

Following the ship's farewell call this autumn, attention in the city is likely to turn to the next scheduled call by a Cunarder in autumn 2009 when Queen Mary 2 will make her inaugural call to the Mersey.

The Commodore is not alone in believing it will be a momentous day for the city and the port.

"The sheer size of the Queen Mary 2 will dominate the city and leave a lasting impression on all who see her. These impressions will remain in their minds and they will want to share them with others and experience them again. This will make the ship iconic in their minds and she will take over where the QE2 has left off," he says.

As the great Liner's days at sea draw to an end the Commodore believes many will be sorry to see her sail into retirement.

"It will be like bereavement," he says.

"Most of us will be very sad but at the same time will be buoyed by many happy memories of our voyages aboard. In our minds will be the consolation that she is not going to a grave but to another lease of life where the opportunity will remain for us to visit her again.

"It's a bit like sending Granny to a care home – we don't want to do it but we know it is the best thing in the long term."

QE2's new owners will take responsibility of the Liner's unique collection of artefacts.

"Ideally, it would be nice for many of the artefacts to remain in the UK, " says the Commodore.

"However, ' he adds, 'it is a very costly exercise to house, maintain and insure valuable items and would involve a lot of time and human resources.

"If items were distributed to museums there is no guarantee that they would remain on display and they could end up in basements or storage units and never see the light of day.

"Hopefully, the collection will remain intact, albeit in another country, and will be there for generations to come."

And like a great many of her loyal guests, officers and crew the Commodore intends to visit QE2 in her new home.

"I would like to continue my association with the ship and hope to visit her in her new role," he says.

Any such visit is sure to be a memorable and emotional occasion for Commodore Warwick.

HOTEL MANAGER JOHN DUFFY CELEBRATES QE2'S WHITE STAR SERVICE

❖ IF GUESTS TRAVELLING ON BOARD QE2 were asked to think of one phrase to sum up their experience in this grandest of floating hotels, many are likely to say it's the attention to detail which sets this ocean liner apart.

Since 1981 responsibility for the overall passenger experience has belonged to QE2 Hotel Manager John Duffy.

It's his team which ensures everything is shipshape everyday. From the fresh flowers throughout the ship's public rooms (not to mention those on sale in the florist's shop on Three Deck) to the exquisite cucumber sandwiches, warm scones and jam served during afternoon tea – QE2's hotel manager oversees every aspect of the guest experience.

After more than 27 years of running the hotel side of the ship John Duffy has an almost unrivalled recollection of the places, people and events which have contributed to QE2's unique history – and her popularity with passengers and fans the world over.

"QE2 was born of a glamorous era where ocean travel still held a mystique for people," he says. "And she was a natural successor to the Queen Mary and Queen Elizabeth which had gone out of service.

"I think that over the years that mystique has stayed with her. And the mystique and reputation of the ship can only stay that way providing the service is top line," explains the Hotel Manger.

And top line service is one of QE2's – and Cunard Line's – hallmarks.

It could also fairly be said that ensuring top line service is achieved and maintained has become a hallmark of John Duffy's entire hotel team.

On the day the announcement of her retirement was made, the Hotel Manger had news of his own for more than 800 crew members under his team's control.

"As soon as the message came through that the ship had been sold, I put the message out that I didn't want to hear any countdowns - six months and three days, six months and two days, five months and eleven days, because I think then the standards would have slipped because naturally if people are like that they are going to ease off.

"I have spoken to the staff and I have said that really what we need and what we want and what we have got to have is for the standard on the last day in Dubai to be as good as the standard on the first day on the maiden voyage.

"We have to keep trying to improve the product right until the end. There can be no letting up. We have got to go out with our heads held high!"

It's a determination – undoubtedly shared by his staff – which the Liverpool-born merchant mariner has used to great affect throughout his career at sea.

The result of his efforts has helped to ensure QE2 remains one of the most highly-rated passenger liners in history.

Retirement in Dubai and the end of the ship's service may beckon but the distinguished Hotel Manager is convinced the emotional farewell should also be a time of celebration.

"People have mixed emotions for the coming months and talk about the farewell and the various functions we have planned, but I tend to think of these times more of a celebration of the QE2's wonderful life because really QE2 is going to a new era, a new phase of her life.

"It's not as though she is going to be scrapped and I think we have to look at these times a as a celebration of her life because she deserves this celebration."

He adds: "I would be far more sad if QE2 did not exist.

"But knowing she is going to be preserved, and long preserved, and she will be open to the public as a museum as well as a hotel and a convention centre, I think is good."

JOHN DUFFY, HOTEL MANAGER, QE2 WITH CUNARD LINE PRESIDENT CAROL MARLOW AFTER RECIEVING TEH MECHANT NAVY MEDAL FOR LONG AND DISTINGUISHED SERVICE

HM THE QUEEN SAYS FAREWELL

ON APRIL 9, 2008,
FOLLOWING AN EARLIER REQUEST FROM BUCKINGHAM PALACE, CUNARD LINE ISSUED A STATEMENT TO THE WORLD'S MAJOR NEWS ORGANISATIONS.

It read:

"Cunard Line is honoured to announce that Her Majesty The Queen will make a farewell visit to Queen Elizabeth 2 in Southampton on Monday, June 2, 2008.

QE2, the most famous ship in the world, and for 35 years the flagship of the Cunard fleet, was launched by Her Majesty at Clydebank on September, 20, 1967 - 40 years ago last year.

"Since then QE2 has travelled more than 5.6 million nautical miles, more than any ship ever; has carried over 2.5 million guests; has completed 25 world cruises; and has crossed the Atlantic 802 times. She leaves Cunard service in November, 2008.

"Her Majesty The Queen has visited QE2 twice since the launch - on May 1, 1969, immediately prior the Maiden Voyage, and on July, 27, 1990 to mark Cunard Line's 150th anniversary.

"Details of the visit on June 2 will be announced shortly, but Cunard's president and managing director, Carol Marlow, comments:

"We are delighted and honoured that The Queen has chosen to visit QE2 to wish her farewell. Her Majesty has taken a close interest in the ship over the last 40 years, and I am certain this will be a memorable occasion for all involved."

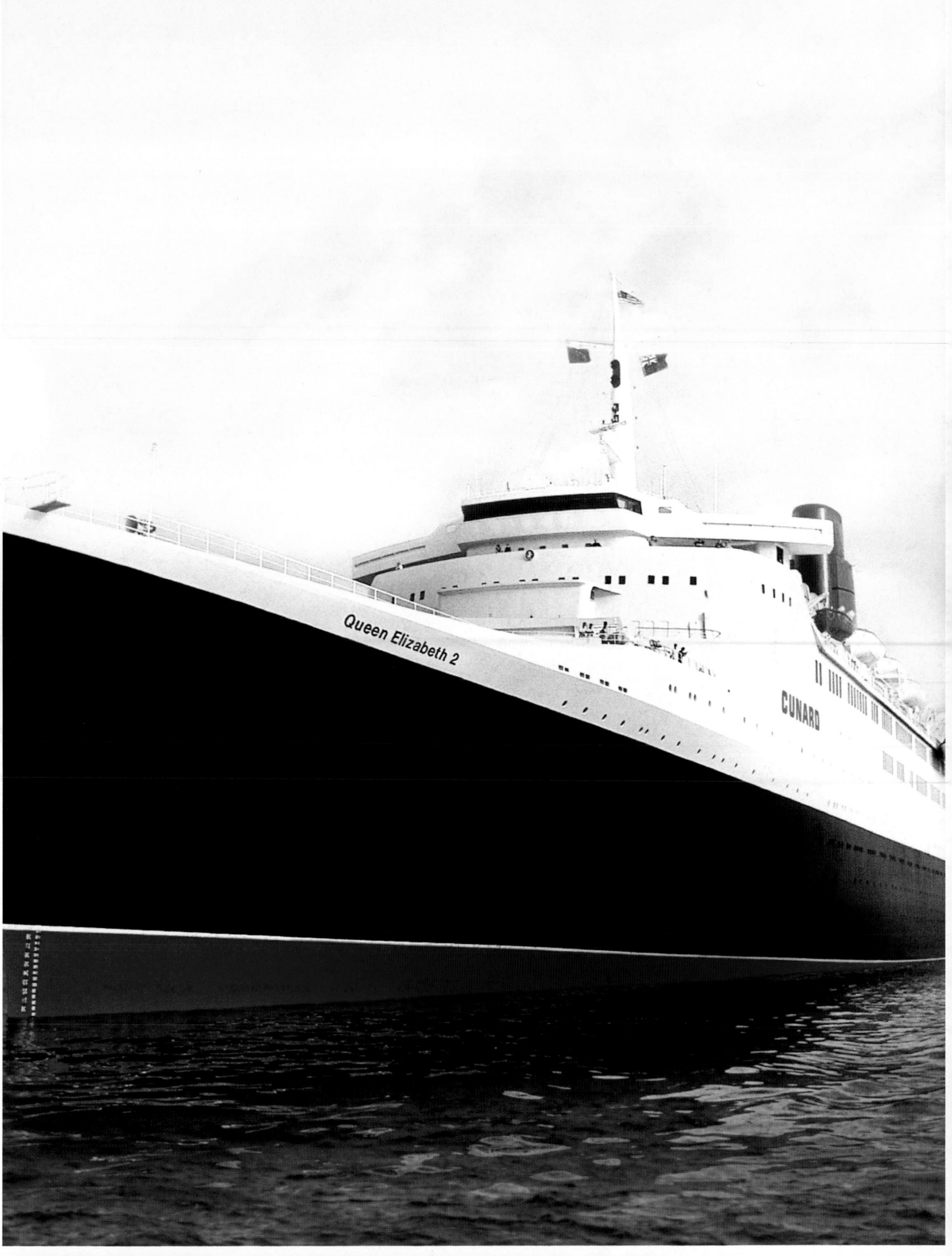
Queen Elizabeth 2
CUNARD

The announcement followed a great deal of advanced planning for what was sure to be a memorable, if at times emotional, Royal farewell to QE2.

Cunard Line and representatives from the Royal Household and Southampton's port operators Associated British Ports had a little under two months in which to prepare for the Queen's visit.

It was to fall on a turn round day for QE2 in her home port.

For the ship's hotel manager John Duffy and his team the task was straightforward: Disembark 1,700 cruise guests and their luggage before the arrival of the Royal Party and more than 200 guests for a private lunch, and before that it's completed and the Royal Party leaves the ship, commence checking in the next 1,700 passengers and their luggage in time for a 5 o'clock departure!

Buckingham Palace officials relayed the Queen's wish to meet as many of the ship's longest-serving crew members as possible during her visit.

One problem the organisers of the visit faced was narrowing down the list of just who would make it into the line ups to be presented to Her Majesty - such has been the length of service and loyalty among officers and crew.

Finally, the lists were agreed together with details of other brief engagements for the Queen during her time on board.

These included signing the Visitors Book in the Ward Room and sitting fro a formal photograph with Captain Ian McNaught and other serving and retired Masters of QE2.

The ship berthed shortly after sunrise at Southampton's Queen Elizabeth II terminal on the morning of Monday, July 2. She would sail again in a little over 12 hours. But what a day it promised to be!

The Royal Party landed in a helicopter of The Queen's Flight at Southampton Airport near Eastleigh and transferred by Royal motorcade to Dock Gate No 4 and the QEII terminal.

After introductions to port officials the group was welcomed by Cunard Line president and managing director Carol Marlow who introduced the Queen to her hosts for the visit, led by Captain McNaught.

After touring the ship the Royal Party arrived in the Queens Room where guests had gathered for a reception before the Queen's arrival.

Carol Marlow addressed the gathering: "Your Majesty, it's with great pleasure that I welcome you all aboard QE2 today.

"It was just over 40 years ago that Your Majesty first saw QE2 - in fact you flew over the ship from above when you were on your way to launch QE2 the new flagship of the British merchant fleet. That was quite some time ago, the September 20, 1967.

"Since then Your Majesty, you have been on board twice to visit the ship but I think this, your fourth visit, may be particularly poignant as Your Majesty bids farewell to this

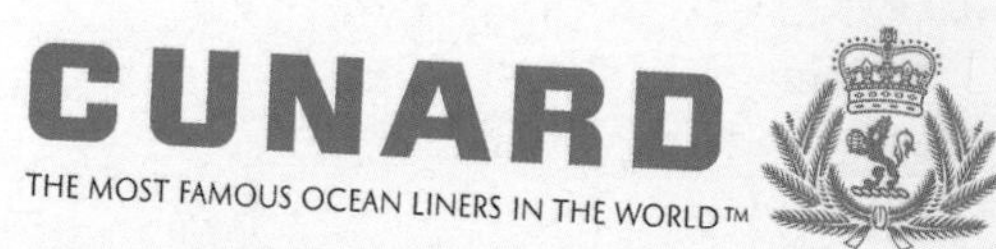

THE ISLE OF MAN POST OFFICE PRODUCE A SPECIAL COMMEMORATIVE COVER TO RECORD THE QUEEN'S FAREWELL

wonderful ship you launched so long ago.

"We are delighted to have you back on board. Thank you for coming one last time and especially on this very particular day of June 2, which is the 55th anniversary of Your Majesty's Coronation. Thank you so much. All of us at Cunard are delighted that you are here today.

"As we all know QE2 is really a symbol of all that is best about Britain. She is quite simply the most famous ship afloat and possibly the most successful liner of all time. But, of course, all things must move on. Cunard has built new liners, Queen Mary 2, Queen Victoria and a new Queen Elizabeth now on the way.

"So QE2's seagoing service will end in November of this year when she goes off to a new home in Dubai to be admired by generations to come.

"QE2 will undoubtedly be missed throughout Britain but especially she will be missed here in her home port of Southampton, the port whose name she has carried around the world for the last 40 years and the port into which she will have berthed 730 times by the time her service finishes.

"So, in order to celebrate QE2's long association with Southampton, Cunard has commissioned notable maritime artist Robert Lloyd to paint the definitive portrait of QE2 here in her home port.

"This painting we intend to present to the people of the City of Southampton in November when QE2 leaves for the last time and we hope that they will see that as a fitting and permanent reminder of their most celebrated liner. Your Majesty, may I ask you to unveil our portrait."

The Royal Party and guests transferred to QE2's Caronia Restaurant for lunch.

On behalf of Cunard Line, Captain McNaught and his officers and crew, Carol Marlow presented The Queen with a framed photograph of the moment she launched QE2 into the Clyde on September 20, 1967.

The Royal Party left the ship later than scheduled with aides letting it be known that Her Majesty had very much enjoyed her opportunity to meet long serving officers and crew as well as bid her own very special farewell to the liner she launched to become the most famous ship in the world.

QE2 FACTS AND FIGURES

Often dubbed a floating hotel, QE2 is in fact far more like a complete city at sea.
QE2 is eight times longer than the Statue of Liberty is high (111 feet), three times as long as Big Ben (310 feet), as long as 30 double-decker London buses (31½ feet each), more than twice as long as St Paul's Cathedral (366 feet), and only 21 feet shorter than the height of the Eiffel Tower (984 feet).
Other facts and figures from this floating city include:

PASSENGER CAPACITY: 1787
DECKS: 13
PASSENGER DECKS: 12
LIFTS: 13 Passenger, 2 (former) Car, 8 Store, 1 Engine Room

CONSUMPTION AND STORES

	DAILY	ANNUALLY
Tea Bags	2,500 bags	912,500 bags
Coffee	100 lbs	16.5 tons
Cooking oil	50 gallons	18,250 gallons
Eggs	3,200	1,168,000
Milk	230 gallons	83,950 gallons
Butter	350 lbs	58 tons
Breakfast cereal	770 packets	281,050 packets
Marmalade / jam	553 portions	201,050 portions
Bananas	230 lbs	38 tons
Strawberries	125 lbs	20 tons
Fruit juice	640 gallons	233,600 gallons
Tomatoes	120lbs	43,800 lbs
Smoked salmon	30 kilos	11 tons
Caviar	6.6 lbs	2,409 lbs
Lobster	116 lbs	42,340 lbs
Strip loin	450 lbs	164,250 lbs
Flour	753 lbs	122 tons
Rice	380 lbs	62 tons
Potatoes	694 lbs	62 tons
Saffron	1.5 packets	547.5 packets
Beer	2,400 bottles	5,309 gallons
Spirits	180 litres	65,700 litres
Champagne	200 bottles	73,000 bottles
Wine	370 bottles	135,050 bottles
Soft drinks	820 bottles	299,300 bottles
Cigarettes	1000 packets	365,000 packets
Cigars	41 boxes	12,425 boxes
Doilies		Over 2 million
Napkins and Cocktail Stirrers		Over 1 million each
Alumium Foil		125 miles

- QE2 sends all its used cooking oil ashore for reconstituting into animal feed.
- 277,000 metres of cling film is used very year, enough to go around the Queen Elizabeth 2 nearly 731 times.
- Heineken and Becks together account for almost 50% of the beer consumed.
- Pound for pound, the most expensive food item on board is saffron (2.5 times the value of Beluga caviar).
- The number of tea bags used each day would supply a family for an entire year.
- To eat QE2's daily consumption of breakfast cereal, two people would have to eat at least one packet a day for more than a year.
- Enough fruit juice is used in one year to fill up QE2's swimming pools nearly 8 times.
- Approximately 600,000 litres of beverage are consumed annually.
- If all the cigarettes smoked annually on board (6.5 million) were placed in a line, the line would be 370 miles long which is equivalent to the distance from London to Edinburgh.
- On a six-day transatlantic crossing, the following beverages are consumed:
  Gin - 600 bottles (7 brands), Rum - 240 bottles (5 brands), Vodka - 129 bottles (3 brands), Brandy - 240 bottles (10 brands), Liqueurs - 360 bottles (18 types), Sherry - 240 bottles (5 brands), Port - 120 bottles (4 brands), Fruit Juice - 25,720 cans

ACCOMMODATION

PASSENGER STATEROOMS:

Total number of staterooms:	947
Outside doubles	636
Outside singles	32
Inside doubles	204
Inside singles	75
Staterooms-equipped for disabled passengers	4

QUEEN MARY AND QUEEN ELIZABETH GRAND SUITES

QE2's two ultra-luxurious 'Grand Suites', named after the most illustrious Cunarders, are among the largest andmost lavish suites afloat. Each 1,184-square foot Grand Suite was decorated in creams, beiges, light woods and feature a bedroom with private veranda, complete with walk-in closet and marble bathroom.

A double door leads to a dining area, which in turn adjoins a raised lounge, leading to a glass-covered conservatory and private, forward-facing deck area.

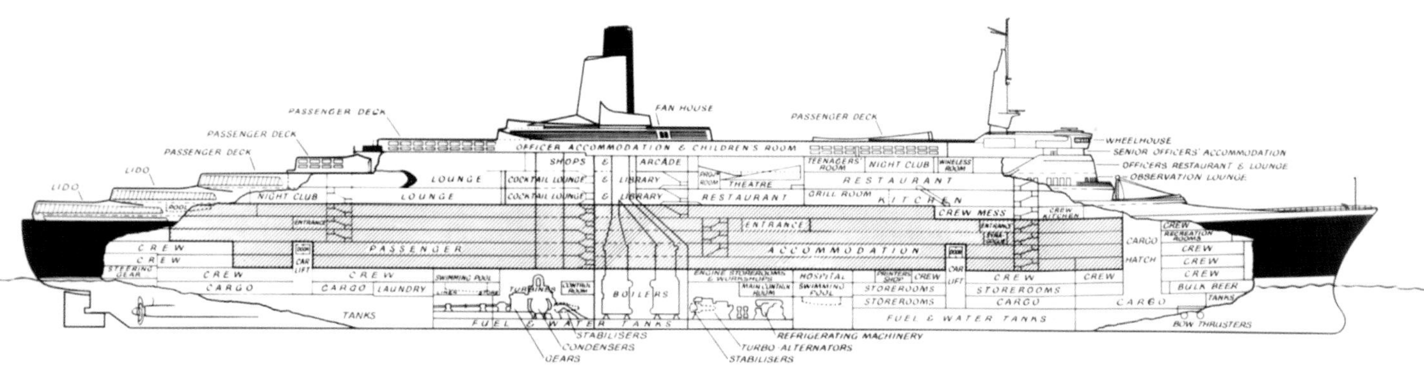

THE SHIP'S COMPANY:

Crew	approximately 1016
Nationality of Officers	Mainly British
Nationality of Staff	International

Captain	1	Fitness Instructors	1
Staff Captain	1	Florists	1
Hotel Manager	1	Gentlemen Hosts	10
Chief Engineer	1	Hairdressers	13
Purser	1	Hotel Officers	35
Cruise Director	1	Kitchen Supervisors	2
Administration Assistant	1	Laundry Staff	17
Assistant Restaurant Managers	12	Librarians	2
Baggage Masters	2	Linenkeeper	1
Bank Staff	3	Lido Supervisor	4
Barkeepers	17	Masters at Arms	4
Beauticians	2	Medical Dispenser	1
Bedroom Stewards/esses	69	Night Stewards	6
Bell Boy	2	Nursery Nurses	2
Bosun	1	Nursing Sisters	3
Bosun's Mate	1	Orchestra Staff	23
Casino Staff	16	Personnel Manager	1
Chefs De Cuisine	5	Photographers	4
Chefs/Sous-Chefs	107	Printers	4
Commis Waiters	13	Public Room Steward/esses	25
Crew Administration Assistant	1	Public Room Supervisor	1
Crew Cooks	2	Radio Officers Radio	1
Cruise Sales Manager	2	Officer AssistantsSecurity	3
Cruise Staff	9	Officer	1
Dancers	10	Secretaries	3
Data Input Clerks	5	Shop Assistants	18
Deck Officers	10	Staff Bedroom Steward	6
Deck Ratings	36	Store Managers	3
Deck Supervisors	9	Storekeepers	5
DJ	1	Tour Staff	3
Doctors	2	TV Manager	1
Engineering Officers	26	Utility Staff	182
Engine Ratings	65	Waiters/Waitresses	175
Entertainers	5	Assistant Waiters	9
Executive Chef	1	Wine Stewards/esses	22

General Information

KEEL LAID:	4 July 1965
LAUNCHED:	20 September 1967 by Her Majesty Queen Elizabeth II
BUILT BY:	John Brown and Co. (Clydebank)Ltd, Scotland; later Upper Clyde Shipbuilders
COST:	£8,825,185
MAIDEN VOYAGE:	2 May 1969 Southampton to New York
PORT OF REGISTRY:	Southampton, England.
SIGNAL LETTERS:	G.B.T.T.
OFFICIAL NUMBER:	336703

Vital Statistics

TONNAGES

Gross:	70,327
Net:	37,182
Deadweight:	11,590

LENGTHS

Overall:	963 feet (293.53 metres)
Bridge to Stem:	282 feet 2.5 inches (86 metres)
Bridge to Stern:	724 feet10 inches (220 metres)
BREADTH:	105 feet 2.5 inches (32.06metres)
DRAUGHT:	32 feet 7.5 inches (9.94 metres)

HEIGHTS

Mast head above Keel:	200 feet 1.5 inches (61 metres)
Funnel above Keel:	204 feet 1.5 inches (62.2 metres)
Masthead above Sea Level:	167 feet 1 inch (51.054mmetres)
Funnel:	69 feet 6 inches (21.2 metres)
Bridge Height of Eye:	95 feet (29 metres)

SPEED

Maximum	32.5 knots
Service	25 - 28.5 knots

FUEL CONSUMPTION
18.05 tonnes per hour, or 433 tonnes per day.

- This is equal to six of the ship's swimming pools.
- The ship's fuel oil tank capacity of 4,381.4 tonnes is sufficient for 10 days' sailing at 32.5 knots, equalling 7,800 miles.
- One gallon of fuel will move the ship 49.5 feet; with the previous steam turbine engines, one gallon of fuel moved the ship 36 feet.

TANK CAPACITIES

Fresh Water	1,852.0 tonnes
Laundry Water	489.0 tonnes
Diesel Oil	206.8 tonnes
Fuel Oil	4,381.4 tonnes
Lubricating Oil	335.7 tonnes
Ballast	4,533.0 tonnes
Feed Water	113.8 tonnes

WATER PRODUCTION / CONSUMPTION

- Four Serck vacuum flash evaporators, producing 250 tonnes each per day.
- One reverse osmosis plant producing 450 tonnes.
- Total production - 1,450 tonnes per day.
- Consumption - about 1,000 tonnes per day; equivalent to 14 of the ship's swimming pools.

STOPPING CAPABILITY

- The ship can reduce speed from 32.5 knots full ahead to standstill in 3 minutes 39 seconds, in a distance of 0.75 autical miles (1.39 km).
- The ship can go from standstill to full speed astern (19 knots) in 12 minutes.

Exterior

THE FUNNEL
This is the most recognisable feature of QE2, the funnel is 69 feet high and is one of the most efficient and practical designs in any passenger liner.

THE MAST

The mast structure performs the useful functions of clearing waste gases from the main kitchen, and carries the radar canners, aerials and navigation lights.

And finally...QE2 has:

- 2,252 light fixtures in passenger areas
- 74,200 square yards of chair and curtain fabric
- 1,350 portholes
- 577 windows
- The most powerful propulsion plant on a non- military vessel
- The most extensive medical facilities after a hospital ship

40TH ANNIVERSARY LAP OF HONOUR

A 40TH BIRTHDAY LAP OF HONOUR AROUND the British Isles was always going to provide another chapter in the unique history of QE2.

Few embarking at her home port of Southampton on Saturday, September 15, 2007, could begin to imagine the experience they were about to share over the next seven days.

Senior figures in the hierarchy of Cunard's parent company Carnival UK had expressed some doubt about the attractiveness of a round Britain itinerary to guests. Eventually, when the voyage was agreed and put on sale, it soon sold out and a waiting list was opened.

CUNARD
Queen Elizabeth 2
40TH
ANNIVERSARY
1967-2007
CUNARD
Queen Elizabeth 2
YARM CROSS

A special lunch was organised on board to mark the departure day. Guest of honour was Baroness Thatcher, returning to the ship which her government took out of service for war duties in the South Atlantic.

Other guests dining in the Caronia Restaurant that day included a host of celebrities from the arts, media and entertainment worlds whose long and fond associations with QE2 have added colourful chapters to the ship's unique history.

Following lunch, guests not sailing stepped ashore - with a little persuasion - as the final passengers completed their embarkation.

Those lucky enough to be travelling took to the open decks of their favourite ship as she edged away from the Queen Elizabeth II terminal.

The band of Her Majesty's Royal Marines struck up for a rousing send off and a 40th birthday party quite unlike any other was underway.

In the course of the voyage, QE2 was to make her inaugural call on the Tyne birthplace of many fine Cunard liners - anchor beneath the mighty Forth Bridge at South Queensferry, near Edinburgh, and return to the river of her birth 40 years to the day the Queen named her, and sent her down the slipway and into the River Clyde at John Brown's shipyard.

The final port of call on this very special itinerary was to Cunard Line's spiritual home at Liverpool.

QE2 was to participate in the Royal opening of the city's long awaited cruise liner berth on the world-famous World Heritage Site Pier Head waterfront and close to Cunard Building, the line's former headquarters.

Under the hazy sunshine of the early evening, QE2 set off down Southampton Water as she had done many hundreds of times during the previous 40 years.

Once again the departure of the great liner from her home port of Southampton was to mark the start of a very special voyage.

After navigating the busy shipping lanes the English Channel and the Dover Straits, QE2 sailed on through the night.

By day break the following day the ship was in the North Sea and preparing for some 'coastal voyaging' along the Yorkshire coast between the Humber and Tyneside.

Crowds were expected along the coast – especially along the promenades and cliff tops of the famous Yorkshire resorts of Flamborough, Filey, Scarborough, Robin Hood's Bay and Whitby.

"QE2 was to participate in the Royal opening of the city's long awaited cruise liner berth on the world-famous World Heritage site Pier Head waterfront and close to the Cunard Building, the line's former headquarters."

Passengers lined every vantage point of QE2's port side as Captain Ian McNaught took his ship close to the shore. Dozens of small craft including RNLI Lifeboats, fishing boats, pleasure cruisers, sailing yachts and even jet skiers bobbed about the great liner. Overhead helicopters and light aircraft flew TV camera crews and photographers over the scene, capturing images of the evening bulletins and the morning newspapers.

Ashore, daylight fireworks and maroons were ignited along the promenades to sound a rousing salute to the most famous ship in the world.

Onboard, preparations were being made to embark one more passenger for the 40th anniversary lap of honour.

Rarely has this great fan of QE2 taken a conventional route through life and today was to be no exception for Sir Jimmy Savile.

Far below the port side bridge wing of QE2 his small fishing boat was edging closer to the liner. Crew had lowered a rope ladder from an open hatch normally used by pilots embarking or disembarking the ship.

Strong winds and a swell rolled the fishing boat to and from the side of the ship. Radio contact had been established between the

crew of the boat and QE2's bridge. They had to decide the best time to transfer the flamboyant passenger.

In the best traditions of Jim'll Fix It, Captain McNaught did his best to make the event memorable and entertaining, slowing his liner to a crawl so Sir Jimmy could jump for the rope ladder and haul himself aboard.

The transfer was completed safely, save a few bangs and bruises to the entertainer's frame. He may have been battered against the side of the ship but his ego was intact.

Later that afternoon another highlight of the tour was to be marked by the arrival at Newcastle, a particularly poignant call for Captain McNaught and his family whose home is in Northumberland.

Previously, a scheduled visit by QE2 to the Tyne was aborted due to poor weather.

Few on board this breezy Sunday

afternoon were aware of that disappointment as QE2 made her way up the coast towards the famous quays marking the mouth of the Tyne.

Ashore, thousands had gathered at coastal vantage points and along the banks of the river to witness QE2's historic maiden arrival. VIP's had been wined and dined as they waited in a marquee on the new cruise liner berth to be inaugurated by QE2 and named by her Master.

Three or so miles off shore, on QE2's bridge, the lavish lunch and naming ceremony were far from the captain's mind as he consulted with the Port of Tyne pilot over their approach to the quays and passage up the Tyne.

Strong winds were getting stronger.

On QE2's open decks passengers were struggling to find shelter but remained determined to stay outside for fear of missing some small part of the arrival.

After agreeing their course, the captain and the pilot positioned QE2 for her entry to the Tyne. As the ship headed towards the quays, crosswinds became fierce, and the approach was abandoned, forcing the ship to turn and head back out to sea to reposition for a second attempt.

A local lifeboat, keeping abreast of QE2 throughout, bobbed about like a cork in the lee of the liner. Powerful tugs waited at the entrance of the river ready to nudge and assist.

For a second time, QE2 was lined up for her approach and for a second time it was abandoned as the winds across her bows became too strong.

"Rarely has this great fan of the QE2 taken a conventional route through life and today was to be no exception for Sir Jimmy Saville."

She turned to regroup out to sea and try a third time.

Hundreds of passengers remained out on QE2's open decks despite the howling winds. On the bridge, wings officers could be seen conferring via radio contact with authorities ashore.

Time and tide were passing. Before too long, regardless of whether the wind subsided or not, there may not have been enough water underneath QE2 to allow her safe entrance to the river.

Under a darkening sky, and after torrential showers whipped by the wind, QE2 was lined up for another approach. Extra tugs had arrived on the scene and took up position.

"Ashore, thousands had gathered at coastal vantage points and along the banks of the river to witness the QE2's arrival."

QE2 headed for the point midway between the quays and finally passed through and into the Tyne for the first time in her history.

After waiting 40 years, Tynesiders were happy to wait a further few hours before launching their own welcome, partying full swing with fireworks, streamers, klaxons, horns and maroons forming a cacophony of sound which bounced off the sides of the ship as she made her triumphant way up the river.

It was almost dark by the time QE2 was safely alongside and Captain McNaught was able to step ashore and officiate at the naming of the new Northumbrian Quay. Along the perimeter fence at the berth, hundreds of onlookers gathered to take in the majestic sight of the floodlit liner.

From dawn the following morning, roads around the pier were clogged with traffic as motorists on their way to work detoured to get a view of the ship.

Children stopped to look on their way to school and later in the day organised school parties descended on the berth with their teachers to learn more about the ship.

Local media organisations were also out in force. Radio and TV trucks broadcast news and images live from the quayside, while special editions of the morning Newcastle Journal and Evening Chronicle were being snapped up by locals and passengers alike.

Just 24 hours after QE2 had finally arrived in the Tyne it was time for her to leave. Thousands of well-wishers once again lined the river as the mighty liner completed a spectacular 360 degree turn off her berth and headed down the river towards the breakwaters.

There, another huge firework display was ignited to send the ship on her way to the country of her birth – Scotland.

"Children stopped to look on their way to school and later in the day organised school parties descended to learn more."

By dawn the following day the QE2 was ready to drop anchor off South Queensferry on the Firth of Forth, a short journey from Edinburgh and the final resting place of another historic British vessel, the Royal Yacht Britannia.

QE2's tenders ferried guests to and from the shore at South Queensferry, passing beneath the mighty Forth Bridge to reach their jetty.

After the thrilling excitement of arriving and departing Newcastle, Edinburgh's contribution to the 40th birthday bash was a positively muted affair. On this occasion at least Glasgow was to play the ace in terms of pomp and ceremony.

After a leisurely day cruising through Pentland Firth and The Minch, during which a passing Air Sea Rescue helicopter dropped off another visitor for a very brief training exercise visit, QE2 set a course for the Clyde and an historic return to Greenock.

Thursday, September, 20, 1967 was one of the most momentous days in a long and distinguished history of shipbuilding on the Clyde.

Forty years to the day that Her Majesty Queen Elizabeth named QE2 and sent her down the John Brown slipway and into water for the first time, the mighty liner, now with almost six million nautical miles on her clock, returned to salute the town that built her.

Excitement and pride ran in equal measure through the town of Greenock. Schools were closed or closing early. Banners and bunting criss-crossed the streets and every other shop window had a QE2 themed display.

The RAF Red Arrows, like Concorde long associated with QE2, were booked to play their own spectacular part in the 40th birthday bash with a display over the Clyde that morning.

By the time the leading pilot's voice crackled over the PA system and the glistening Hawk jets roared into view trailing

their trademark red, white and blue smoke, thousands of spectators were gathered to witness the display.

On board, every square foot of open deck space was occupied by passengers, crew members and guests - including former John Brown workers who had helped build her - eyes skywards for a glimpse of the display.

One excited crew member with a spectator point close to the ship's mighty brick-red funnel later recounted seeing the planes pass beneath his vantage point.

Even by Red Arrows' standards it has been a stunning display - unusually completed with eight rather than the customary nine aircraft after a technical hitch struck one pilot as he joined colleagues on the flight north from the Arrows' base.

After the display, those on board enjoyed another celebration lunch and, as the time ticked towards 2.28pm, the precise 40th anniversary of the QE2's naming by HM The Queen, the officer of the watch on the bridge prepared to sound the ship's distinctive whistle for 40 seconds.

Cheers were long and loud and glasses were charged and raised as the birthday hour passed.

"New Brighton was packed solid with people, and all the way up, Seacombe, Woodside and the Pier Head were packed with crowds of spectators."

After an afternoon of such excitement there was barely time to prepare for the departure from Greenock early that evening. Hundreds of boats, dinghies, yachts, pleasure craft and other vessel crowded around QE2 as she set off for Liverpool.

Glasgow had become the latest call on this most memorable of voyages. Liverpool was next.

QE2's first visit to the River Mersey, in July, 1990 as part of the 150th anniversary of the founding of the line by Sir Samuel Cunard, attracted one million spectators. It was a day blessed with clear skies and fine sunshine from dawn until dusk.

By contrast, Friday, September, 21, 2007, was wet.

As QE2 crossed the Mersey Bar before dawn, visibility through low cloud, mist and driving rain was extremely poor. On the open deck beneath the bridge, passengers hoping for an early glimpse of Liverpool's famous Three Graces - including the Cunard Building - were disappointed.

And, instead of cheers from well-wishers lining the shore, all they could hear were the windscreen wipers struggling to keep a view through the bridge windows.

Had the weather been kinder, those on board would have had an early view of Liverpool's new cruise liner terminal which was to be officially opened during QE2's day in the city.

For most on board though, the highlight of this day, and the entire week long voyage, was to be a special celebration concert at the Anglican Cathedral.

Welcomes by the city's then Lord Mayor Cllr Paul Clark and Bishop James Jones marked the start of a moving and memorable thanksgiving for QE2, punctuated by stirring solo performances by soprano Lesley Garrett and tenor Nicky Spence.

Celebration Concert At The Cathedral

FRIDAY 21 SEPTEMBER 2007

featuring

Lesley Garrett CBE

Nicky Spence

The Royal Liverpool Philharmonic Orchestra and Choir

The Liverpool Cathedral Choir

The Band of the Scots Guards

under the direction of

Lieutenant Colonel RJ Owen MA, ARCM psm

Senior Director of Music – Guards Division

Organist: Professor Dr Ian Tracey

Conductor: Anthony Inglis

The musical programme was interspersed with short addresses to the audience. In one, Baroness Thatcher's broadcaster and journalist daughter Carol, who was sailing on board for the week, told guests:

"For many people, QE2 conjures up images of exotic voyages, excellent service and fabulous food.

"She certainly does that for me.

But she also conjures up memories of her role in the Falklands War, which was a tense and turbulent time for my family, as it was for many others.

"I well remember surprise being expressed when my mother sanctioned the requisition of QE2 for service in the war. There was concern that the loss of such a notable British icon, such a high-profile symbol of what is best about Britain, would be a huge blow to public morale. And certainly my mother is on record as saying that she never

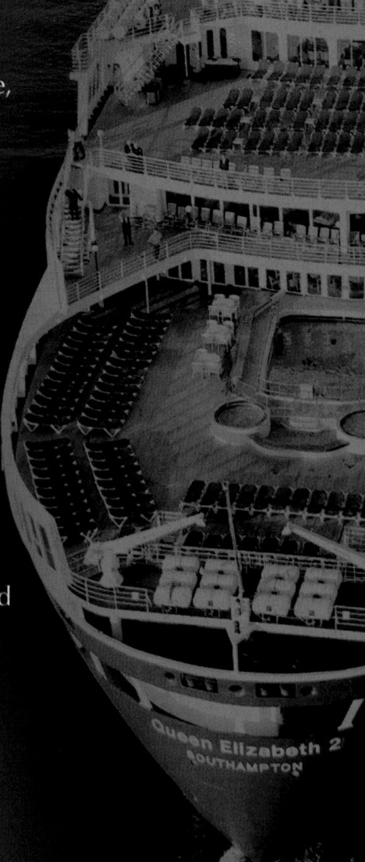

had so many sleepless nights as prime minister as she did during the weeks the liner was journeying to the South Atlantic.

"But, of course, there was no choice. No other ship could have carried so many, so far, so fast.

"Few of us will forget her emotional return on June, 11, 1982, when she sailed into Southampton bearing the survivors of HMS Coventry, Antelope and Ardent and was saluted by The Queen Mother on board the Royal Yacht Britannia.

"And few will forget the day she sailed out of Southampton, May, 12, 1982 - having been converted in just eight days into a troop ship, and carrying to the theatre of war the 3,000 troops of the Fifth Infantry Brigade made up of the Welsh Guards, the Gurkha Rifles and, of course, the magnificent men of the Scots Guards."

The final words of her address from the pulpit were cue for the Band of the Scots Guards to march into the cathedral in a stirring entrance down the aisle.

Before the finale, Captain McNaught told those assembled:

"Today, together, we have celebrated the long and extraordinary life of a great ocean liner. An ocean liner which was conceived and planned here in Liverpool. So far, QE2 has visited Liverpool - which was Cunard's home for 128 years - eight times.

But the next time, the ninth time, will be the last time.

After that, she will not pass this way again."

His words reminded those present that the liner's future had been decided.

After all the adventures and achievement of her 40 years in service being celebrated during her voyage around Britain, retirement finally beckoned.

Queen Mary 2

SISTER SHIPS

WHEN QE2 FINALLY LEAVES THE UK FOR THE LAST TIME IN NOVEMBER BOUND FOR RETIREMENT IN DUBAI, SHE WILL LEAVE BEHIND TWO OF THE MOST STRIKING CUNARDERS EVER TO SAIL IN THE FLEET SINCE ITS CREATION 168 YEARS AGO. QUEEN MARY 2 AND QUEEN VICTORIA MAY NOT YET HAVE THEIR PLACE FIRMLY ESTABLISHED IN THE AFFECTIONS OF MANY OF CUNARD LINE'S LONG-LOYAL GUESTS. BUT THEY ARE DESTINED TO TAKE THEIR OWN PLACE IN CUNARD LINE HISTORY.

QUEEN MARY 2 - A CITY AT SEA

The mighty Queen Mary 2 took over as flagship of the fleet when she was named by HM Queen Elizabeth II during a stunning ceremony in Southampton early in 2004.

Queen Mary 2 entered service on January 12, 2004 and made worldwide headlines. Queen Mary 2 is the first transatlantic liner to be built since QE2 and is the only liner offering a scheduled transatlantic service between Europe and North America.

Queen Mary 2 is the biggest (151,400-tons), the longest (1,132ft/342m), the tallest (236ft/72m) the widest (135ft/41m) passenger liner ever and, at a cost of £540 million, was, on entering service, the most expensive passenger ship in history.

Queen Mary 2 quickly established herself as a destination in her own right. There is over £3.5 million of artwork on board. The world's first floating Planetarium offers virtual reality rides through the galaxy.

She has the first suites with private lift access, the first Canyon Ranch Spa at sea, the first Veuve Clicquot Champagne Bar at sea (Queen Victoria has the second!), the largest library at sea (with 8,000 hardbacks, 500 paperbacks, 200 audio books and 100 CD ROMs) and the largest ballroom with the biggest dance floor at sea.

Workshops and master classes are performed by RADA (the Royal Academy of Dramatic Arts). She also boasts the longest jogging track at sea, the largest and most extensive wine cellar at sea - and, if that's not enough, the 'Queen Mary 2' signs near the funnel are the largest illuminated ship's name signs in maritime history!

First impressions matter and Queen Mary 2 impresses as soon as guests embark into the ship's six-storey Grand Lobby which features a dramatic staircase and exclusive works of art.

Just as aboard her sister QE2, each grade of stateroom is paired with a sea-view restaurant where the occupants dine during the voyage.

The restaurants follow a similar pattern to that provided on QE2, with Grill Rooms for the higher categories and restaurants for deluxe and standard.

The main Dining Room, the Britannia Restaurant (seating 1,347 guests), is one of the most remarkable rooms at sea, spanning the full width of the ship and nearly three storeys in height with tiered dining on two levels.

The Britannia Restaurant evokes memories of classic ocean liner restaurants with a sweeping central staircase – perfect for those who wish to make a grand entrance – an overhead light well and classic columns.

A vast tapestry of a past Cunard liner hangs as a centrepiece.

Decorated in gold, the 200-seat Queen's Grill is for the use of guests booked in the highest-grade staterooms and features the finest dining afloat. These guests will also have the exclusive use of the Queen's Grill Bar (conveniently located next to the Grill) and Queen's Grill Terrace on deck.

The intimate 178-seat Princess Grill, decorated in silver, is for guests in the Junior Suite staterooms.

In addition Queen Mary 2 offers several alternative dining venues:

The Todd English Restaurant on Deck 8 offers innovative Mediterranean cuisine in a modern setting. The room has been designed with intimate alcoves and architectural detailing and overlooks the Pool Terrace allowing for al fresco dining (an additional 56 seats).

The informal King's Court serves breakfast and lunch buffet style. Decorated screens transform the area into four different dining venues at night: La Piazza (Italian) - open 24 hours; Lotus (Asian); The Carvery (British); Chef's Galley (Demonstration Kitchen).

The Chef's Galley features a chef giving a live demonstration of the meal preparation that will be broadcast via close circuit TV onto a large screen.

For snacks, the Boardwalk Café offers fast food choices outdoors and even the Golden Lion Pub offers traditional English pub food including fish and chips and steak and ale pie for lunch! Eating is by no means the only onboard experience to enjoy on Queen Mary 2!

As well as some of the finest dining at sea, the ship is home to some spectacular entertainment venues.

The Royal Court Theatre, with tiered seating for more than 1,000 guests, is the location for the main entertainment of the evening with full-scale, West End-style productions and entertainers.

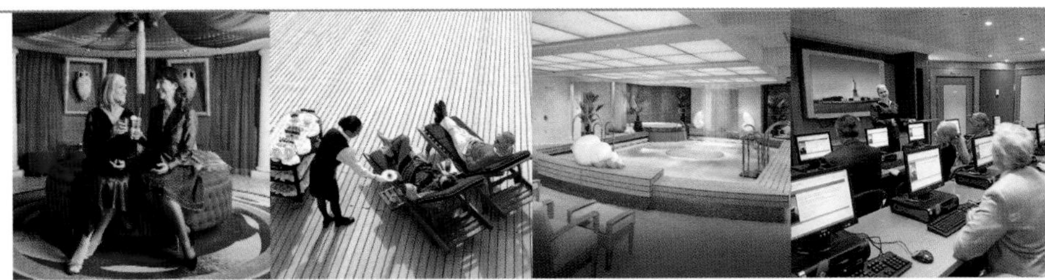

Classically elegant in style, there is a hydraulic proscenium stage and highly sophisticated light and sound equipment as well as excellent sight-lines.

The Queen's Room is the largest ballroom at sea and is designed for ballroom dancing, cocktail parties and afternoon teas. It features a dramatic high ceiling (more than seven metres high), crystal chandeliers, sweeping ocean views on both sides of the ship and the largest dance floor at sea (measuring 7.5m by 13m).

Illuminations acts as cinema/auditorium, lecture hall and broadcast studio. This is also the first planetarium at sea featuring high-tech programmes and virtual reality films.

ConneXions is a unique education centre featuring seven flexible classroom venues for Cunard's College At Sea programme. Classes in everything from computer training, seamanship and navigation to art and wine appreciation, languages and photography are taught by expert instructors during voyages.

The Winter Garden acts as the 'quiet area' and is reminiscent of a grand conservatory with flowers in bloom all year long, aroma management, a large waterfall and a piano.

Queen Mary 2 offers a whole range of bars and clubs (14 in total) to suit a wide variety of tastes and provide a range of atmospheres, including a traditional English Pub (the Golden Lion), an up-market modern Wine Bar (Sir Samuel's), a nautically-themed cocktail bar (The Chart Room) and the Veuve Clicquot Champagne Bar.

Outside there is a Terrace Bar and Regatta Bar.

The state of the art Empire Casino features the latest machines, traditional tables and an accompanying bar while the Mayfair Shops offer eight different shops including boutiques from Chanel, Hermes and Dunhill.

The G32 Nightclub is named after the hull number given to the ship by the shipyard at St Nazaire in Brittany where she was built.

G32 nightclub is strategically situated overlooking the stern of the ship - away from guest cabins!

The forward Commodore Club observation lounge found on deck 9 offers sweeping views over the bow of Queen Mary 2 and features jazz each evening. Connected to this room are the Boardroom and Cigar Lounge.

The library and bookshop is the largest to be found at sea, luxuriously appointed with leather sofas and armchairs.

Children have not been forgotten and facilities on board Queen Mary 2 are among the finest afloat.

The Play Zone and The Zone have the latest equipment for children of all ages, a permanent staff and nursery nurses.

Children have their own dedicated pool and inside/outside play area.

'Drive-In' movies (with popcorn) can be staged on Deck 12 by the Boardwalk Café.

For those interested in the history of Cunard, 'Maritime Quest' is a museum quality audio tour that tells the story of the most famous name in shipping.

Health and fitness facilities are among the largest and most extensive ever to be featured on board a ship. The Queen Mary 2 Canyon Ranch Spa offers services previously only found in luxurious, spas ashore, and is of such quality that some guests choose to sail on the ship for its spa facilities alone!

Facilities and services include massages and therapeutic bodywork, mud, aromatherapy, ayuvedic and seaweed treatments, facials and masks, conditioning body scrubs and therapeutic body cocoons.

There is also a complete gymnasium, Thalassotherapy pool, whirlpool, herbal sauna, Finnish sauna, reflexology basins and an aromatic steam room.

There is a £3.5 million art collection on display throughout Queen Mary 2. Renowned international artists were commissioned to produce more than 300 works of art displayed on board.

Other than the large indoor pool in the Spa, there are four swimming pools outside. One of these can be covered by a retractable sliding glass roof

There is a large sunning area with a sports bar. Towering more than 200ft above sea level the sports facilities include two state-of-the-art golf simulators, a half-size basketball court, putting green, quoits, shuffleboard, deck games, a giant chess board and a paddle tennis court. There are eight whirlpool tubs.

Another classic feature is the expansive Promenade Deck, recreating an area which always served an important social function aboard transatlantic liners.

This deck allows a 360° passage around the ship, protected from the weather at the forward end.

The Promenade circuit is approximately 645 yards (580m) with one lap being just over one third of a mile. This generous deck can accommodate a line of full-length wooden steamer chairs, and still leave room for guests walking four abreast to pass between the seated guests and the rail.

The medical facility is one of the largest and most modern of its kind afloat.

Other shipboard amenities include a beauty salon, currency exchange bank, dry cleaning /valet service, 22 lifts and a florist.

Queen Mary 2 is a city at sea in every respect!

Queen Victoria, named by the Duchess of Cornwall at Southampton in December, 2007, is the newest ship in the Cunard fleet.

QUEEN VICTORIA - THE NEWEST RECRUIT

Despite being relatively new to service, this classically appointed vessel has quickly established herself as a favourite alternative to QE2 for many Cunard Line regulars.

Queen Victoria is larger than QE2 - but smaller than Queen Mary 2 with a size and layout which many first-time guests are finding is to their liking.

The liner design of Queen Victoria has provided the ship's interior designers with more space in terms of height and volume.

Queen Victoria's Cunard heritage is reflected in the design of the grand, elegant and intimate public areas.

Guests embark into the ship's three-storey Grand Lobby decorated in mahogany and marble and featuring dramatic staircases with ornate wrought iron balustrade.

A specially-commissioned art work spanning over two decks in height symbolises the Cunard and Victoria historical style, and a dramatic ceiling with a central feature chandelier are the striking focal points of the Grand Lobby.

As on her sister Cunarders, each grade of stateroom is paired with a sea-view restaurant.

The restaurants follow a similar pattern to QE2 and QM2. Grill Rooms are provided for the higher categories and a main restaurant for the deluxe and standard grades.

The main dining room, the Britannia Restaurant, spans two decks at the stern of the vessel, and evokes memories of classic ocean liner restaurants with sweeping staircases, art deco pillars and arches and a spectacular bronze and glass artwork centrepiece.

Both the Queen's and Princess Grills are located on top of the ship with exclusive access to Grill guests only. All Grill guests have the exclusive use of the Grills Lounge, conveniently located next to the Grills, and French doors open from each Grill onto The Courtyard - an exclusive patio area with steps to the Upper Grills Terrace - a secluded retreat on the ship's uppermost deck.

Decorated in creams and browns, the Queen's Grill is used by guests booked in the highest-grade staterooms and feature the fine dining.

The intimate Princess Grill is for guests in the Princess Suite staterooms.

Like QM2, Queen Victoria offers several alternative dining venues: another Todd English Restaurant; the informal Lido; Café Carinthia; the Golden Lion Pub will offer traditional English pub food for lunch and a Hamburger and Salad Bar

Queen Victoria's three-deck Royal Court Theatre offers the first private boxes at sea with a lounge area for guests to enjoy dessert and coffee before being escorted to their box before the show.

The two-deck Queen's Room is the ship's ballroom designed for dancing, cocktail parties and traditional English afternoon teas complete with finger sandwiches

Fencng classes also take place here!

The room features crystal chandeliers, a large dance floor with inlaid wood patterns and backlit glass panels.

ConneXions Conference Centre and Internet Café comprise an education centre featuring a flexible classroom venue for programmes that include computer training, navigation, art and wine tasting.

Subject to satellite availability, The Internet Café enables guests to stay in touch during their voyage as well as surf the web.

With its retractable glass roof, The Winter Garden is Queen Victoria's indoor/outdoor relaxation area and will be reminiscent of a grand conservatory complete with fountain.

Queen Victoria offers a range of bars and clubs (13 in total) to suit a wide variety of tastes and provide a range of atmospheres, including the Golden Lion pub; a Champagne Bar; a nautically-themed cocktail bar (The Chart Room) and the relaxing Midships Lounge.

A modern casino will feature the latest machines, traditional tables and an accompanying bar.

The Royal Arcade shops facility was inspired by both the Royal and Burlington Arcades in London.

Queen Victoria's Hemispheres room on top of the ship, overlooks the Pavilion Pool and is the venue for classes, lectures or just relaxation by day, before being transformed into a stunning nightclub in the evening.

The Commodore Club observation lounge features full bar and sweeping views over the bow of Queen Victoria.

Adjacent to this room is the Admiral's Lounge and Churchill's Cigar Lounge.

The 6,000-book traditionally-styled English Library, situated over two decks features rich mahogany wood panelling, stained glass, leather sofas and armchairs and a spiral staircase. Complementing the library is the bookshop.

Queen Victoria also features a floating museum called Cunardia displaying a

unique collection of Cunard memorabilia and artefacts.

Child facilities on board Queen Victoria are among the finest afloat.

The Cunard Royal Spa and Fitness Centre features the latest spa and beauty treatments for both men and women, as well as a hydro-pool and thermal suite.

Next to the Spa and Treatment Rooms, there's an expansive gymnasium and aerobics area with state-of-the-art cardiovascular fitness equipment including inclining treadmills and bikes complete with their own personal LCD TV screens.

Other than the large hydro-pool in the Spa, there are two outdoor swimming pools.

As her maiden season draws to a close, Queen Victoria is well on the way to becoming a firm favourite among cruise aficionados!

QE2 STAR TRIBUTES

FAMOUS FACES HAVE TRAVELLED the world on board Cunard liners and QE2 has welcomed many of the world's best known heads of state, politicians, sports and screen stars, church leaders and celebrities.

In the 1920s and 1930s, QE2's illustrious sisters put the golden age of steam travel firmly on the map, reminding guests that 'getting there is half the fun.'

Travellers from all walks of life, including royalty and celebrities, were indulged with Cunard Line's famous White Star Service.

In the late swinging sixties QE2 established herself as the preferred form of transatlantic travel for the stars of the day.

Other famous travellers have shared their own view of life on board and the unforgettable experience of sailing on the most famous ocean liner in the world.

DAME BERYL BAINBRIDGE:

"The first time I travelled on the great QE2 was in the company of the late, lamented Marj Proops and the ever lively Jimmy Savile. The latter ran round and round the top deck in his shorts while Marj and I propped up the bar. To sail on such a vessel is to know why Britain was once the envy of the world. The second time I boarded the ship it was to give a talk on the sinking of the Titanic, an event which seemed to go down very well - the talk, not the ship!"

ROY BARRACLOUGH:

"I first discovered her when we filmed a Coronation Street special. I, as Alec Gilroy, was playing her hapless cruise director. We had such a wonderful time - she is rather like a stately home - steeped in history and staffed by the most caring and talented people. But most of all, unlike many more modern vessels, she is very much a ship."

ANGELA RIPPON:

"Whilst in mid Atlantic on an outward bound journey to New York, the captain announced that Concorde would be flying over the liner within the next 10 minutes. What seemed like the entire complement of passengers crowded the decks in anticipation. Then, there she was - Concorde, flying low over the horizon, at normal, not supersonic speed. As she passed over the funnel a huge cheer went up, and QE2 sounded her whistle. The Queen of the Seas saluting the Queen of the Skies. It was a magical moment and definitely one for the 'special memories' file of everyone on board."

"The second time I boarded the ship it was to give a talk on the sinking of the Titanic, an event which seemed to go down very well - the talk, not the ship!"

Dame Beryl Bainbridge

NELSON MANDELA:

"Travelling on QE2 was an unforgettable honour and pleasure."

MICHAEL BUERK:

"I can't believe the QE2 has passed 40. Mind you, I can't believe I am 60. The difference is that this wonderful ship has matured; I have merely aged. I like her for a hundred reasons. Here's two. First, she's a proper liner, built for travellers, a luxury greyhound of the seas for people who want to get places, not just lie around the same bit of ocean all day. She's twice as fast as today's cruise boats, a ship not a floating block of flats. Second, we all have our favourite bits of the ship, the little bar that's the best place for an aperitif, the quiet corner where you can read in the sunshine, the Queen's Grill, an old-fashioned definition of first-class, and the better for it. Which brings me to, third (I know I said two reasons). One word. Tradition."

ESTHER RANTZEN:

"My husband, Desmond Wilcox, ran away to sea when he was 15, and became a sail-training apprentice on the mighty four-masted clipper, Pamia. Then he lied about his age and signed on as a deck-hand on a tramp steamer. He sailed to Africa and back, suffering sunburn on the way out and gangrene on the way back. So when I suggested 50 years later that we two should take a cruise on the QE2 along the Mediterranean, he was scathing. That wasn't sailing as he had known it, the rough, horny-handed, adventures he was used to, chipping the rust off the railings and scaling the heights of the topsail. But he agreed to go to Southampton and take a look. He told me he had been expecting a huge, featureless sea-going block of flats. Instead he found a ship, a real wood and brass, tough but luxurious craft, burnished with love and affection by generations of sailors like him. She may no longer be the biggest, or the fastest ship in the world, but in my eyes the QE2 is still the Queen of the ocean."

Terry Waite:

"It was a lovely sunny afternoon and my wife and I were standing on the deck of QE2 each sipping a glass of Champagne. On the quayside a military band was playing as the crew of this wonderful ship prepared to cast off. This was Southampton and our destination was New York.

Just as the gangway was about to be lifted we heard the sound of a car racing at full speed. A taxi came into sight and screeched to a halt. The driver flung open the door and ran to the boot to collect luggage whilst an elegant couple leapt from the back seat and quickly clambered on board. Within a few moments the last rope was cast off; the band struck up and QE2 set sail down Southampton Water.

Later that night we heard the full story. An American couple were enjoying a holiday in London. Like so many before them they had flown to the UK and were taking QE2 back to their homeland. It was their first visit to England and they enjoyed London so much that on their final morning they decided to take a car to show them more of the sights and then take them to the ship for an afternoon departure. All went well until they arrived at what the driver understood to be their destination. 'Where exactly do you want?' he inquired. 'The docks,' they replied.

Their reply clearly puzzled the driver. 'Docks?' he said, 'I don't know any docks here.'

Alas, the American travellers, unfamiliar with British place names had asked for Northampton in the Midlands and not Southampton some 200 miles away. The driver did a smart about turn and to his credit got to the ship with seconds to spare.

A journey to remember but, as so many say, all journeys on QE2 are journeys to remember."

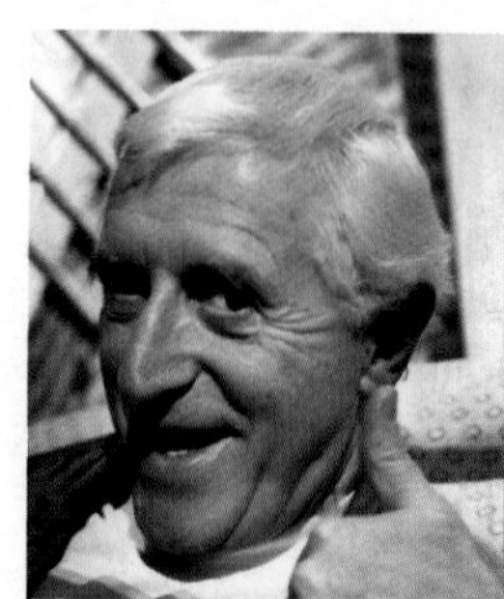

"The world we live in travels continuously at 16,000 miles an hour through space. The QE2 travels continuously at a much more leisurely pace - but it's still a separate world. And what a world."

Sir Jimmy Savile

Leslie Thomas:

"We used to play a sort of game where I would ask for something unusual for dinner the following night and they took pride in being able to provide it. One night I requested Spam, as we knew it during and after the war. The following evening four waiters, led by the maitre d', bore a gigantic silver taureen to the table. With great ceremony the ornate lid was removed and there sat a tin of Spam – US Army rations."

Sir Cyril Smith:

"I made many valued friendships aboard the QE2, which are still maintained and my fondest memory is being on the Bridge (with the captain's permission) and docking the ship in Gibraltar."

Sir Jimmy Savile:

"The world we live in travels continuously at 16,000 miles an hour, through space.

The QE2 travels continuously at a much more leisurely pace – but it's still a separate world. And what a world.

On one cruise - I've done over 40 on the QE2 in total - there was lobster on the menu. As a joke I said to the restaurant manager 'is this from Maine'?

'No sir,' says he, 'but your next one will be.'

Lo and behold, docked in Naples, he announced 'your lobster Sir Jimmy, just flown in from Maine.'

And it had. That's QE2 style."

"I can't believe the QE2 has passed 40. Mind you, I can't believe I am 60. The difference is that this wonderful ship has matured; I have merely aged."
Michael Buerk

Sir Bernard Ingham:

"The QE2 is a real, beautiful ship with a wonderful history in peace and war. It was a delight to return to her with Margaret Thatcher for the 20th anniversary of the Falklands Campaign. The QE2 exudes a sense of history, security and good living."

Baroness James of Holland Park

"No matter what bigger or faster ships may be launched, the QE2 holds a unique place in the affections of those of us fortunate enough to have sailed on her. My own journeys have been the Southampton-New York crossings, voyages which gave an unrivalled opportunity to experience the unostentatious elegance, the superb facilities, the spacious cabins and the wonderful service on what for so many will always remain the most gracious Queen of the ocean liners."

Other Famous Cunard Line Guests on Board QE2 Include:

Members of Royal Families and the Aristocracy Who Have Travelled:

HM The Queen

HRH The Duke of Edinburgh

HRH The Prince of Wales

HRH The Prince Edward

Diana, Princess of Wales

King Hussein of Jordan

The Emperor of Japan

Princess Christine of the Netherlands

Prince Nikita Romanoff

The Sultan of Brunei

The Sultan of Selanghor

The Saudi Royal Family

Earl Mountbatten

Earl of Snowdon

Earl of Lichfield

Lord Wedgwood

Lord Montagu of Beaulieu

Politicians, Diplomats and Churchmen Who Have Travelled:

Lord Archer of Weston-super-Mare

George Bush Jnr

President Jimmy Carter

Edwina Currie

Sir Nicholas Fairbairn

H R Haldeman

Bob Hawke

Sir Rex Hunt

Dame Jill Knight

Mayor John Lindsay

Lee Kuan Yew

Graca Machel

President Nelson Mandela

Lord Mason of Barnsley

Shimon Peres

Dame Stella Rimington

The Most Revd Lord Runcie of Cuddesdon

Sir Cyril Smith

Lord Taylor of Warwick

Eminent People Who Have Visited But Not Travelled:

HM Queen Elizabeth

The Queen Mother

HRH The Prince Andrew

HRH The Princess Royal

Lady Thatcher

Lord Attenborough

Chief Mangosuthu Buthelezi

Mrs Cherie Blair

Mrs Elizabeth Dole

Sir David Frost

Charles Haughey

Albert Reynolds

Earl and Countess Spencer

Rt Hon John Prescott MP

Richard Baker

Chris de Burgh

Lady Ivar Mountbatten

Beverley Craven

Tony Hadley

Katrina and the Waves

Musicians Who Have Travelled:

Moira Anderson

Applejacks

Larry Adler

Charles Aznavour

Count Basie

Dave Berry

John Briggs

Joe Brown

The Cure

Vic Damone

Gracie Fields

Wayne Fontana

Gerry and the Pacemakers

Marvin Hamlisch

George Harrison

Herman's Hermits

Edmund Hockridge

Mick Jagger

Elton John

Davy Jones

Jack Jones

Frankie Laine

Joe Loss

Patti Lupone

Dame Vera Lynn

Maureen McGovern

Harry Neilson

Yoko Ono

Oscar Peterson

Linda Ronstadt

Neil Sedaka

Carly Simon

Ringo Starr

Rod Stewart

Tommy Tune

Frankie Vaughan

Sarah Vaughan

Nancy Wilson

Eminent Journalists and Authors Who Have Travelled:

Fiona Armstrong

Beryl Bainbridge

Lynne Barber

Alan Bleasdale

Carol Barnes

Jennie Bond

Craig Brown

Michael Brunson

Michael Buerk

Paul Burrell

Bill Bryson

Tom Clancy

Matthew Collins

Clive Cussler

Frank Delaney

Colin Dexter

Dick Francis

Sandy Gall

Tim Heald

Hannah Hauxwell

Richard Hendrick

Brian Hitchen

Mary Higgins Clark

Sir Bernard Ingham

Virginia Ironside

Paul Johnson

P D James

Sir Ludovic Kennedy

Roddy Llewellyn

Jackie and Sunny Mann

Brian Masters

Frank McCourt

Angus McGill

James Mitchener

Sheridan Morley

Flt Lt John Nichol

Sir David Nicholas

Pat O'Brien

Anna Pavard

Marje Proops

Claire Rayner

Celia Sandys

Selina Scott

Michael Shea

Mary Ann Sieghart

John Simpson

Peter Sissons

Sir Roy Strong

Carol Thatcher

Leslie Thomas

Jack Tinker

Hugo Vickers

Terry Waite

Tony Warren

Tennessee Williams

Nigel West

Roland White

Stars of Stage and Screen Who Have Travelled:

John Altman

Eamonn Andrews

Julie Andrews

Patrick Anthony

Debbie Arnold

Michael Aspel

Peter Baldwin

Roy Barraclough

Thelma Barlow

Jeremy Beadle

Sean Bean
Isla Blair
Victor Borge
Jim Bowen
Tracy Brabin
Johnny Briggs
George Burns
Richard Burton
James Cagney
Beverly Callard
Jasper Carrott
Cy Chadwick
Judith Chalmers
Petula Clark
Glenn Close
Rosemary Conley
Bill Cosby
Judy Cornwell
Michael Crawford
Jimmy Cricket
Tim Curry
Tony Curtis
Jill Dando
Paul Daniels
Nigel Davenport
Liz Dawn
Les Dawson
Dame Judi Dench
Neil Diamond
Sue Eden
Douglas Fairbanks Jnr
Eddie Fisher
Bryan Forbes
Fiona Fullerton
Susan George
Hermoine Gingold
Lillian Gish
Jilly Goolden
Peter Gordeno
Russell Grant

Hughie Green
Richard Griffiths
Larry Hagman
Stuart Hall
Mona Hammond
Rolf Harris
Lawrence Harvey
Dickie Henderson
Jim Henson
Sherrie Hewson
Geoff Hinsliff
Thora Hird
Bob Holness
Bob Hope
Frankie Howerd
Rock Hudson
Geoffrey Hughes
Lorraine Kelly
Kevin Kennedy
Eric Knowles
Barbara Knox
Robert Kilroy Silk
Kris Kristofferson
Sara Lancashire
Burt Lancaster
Roy Lancaster
Danny LaRue
Christopher Lee
Maureen Lipman
Moira Lister
Emily Lloyd
Deborah Lyttle
Barry Manilow
Dean Martin
Raymond Massey
Nichola McAuliffe
Leo McKern
Hayley Mills
Sir John Mills
Matthew Modine

Bob Monkhouse
Ken Morley
Bryan Mosley
David Neilson
Bob Newhart
Nannette Newman
Paul Newman
Barry Norman
Tom O'Connor
Sid Owen
Patsy Palmer
Nicholas Parsons
John Peal
Dr Mark Porter
Robert Powell
Vincent Price
Charley Pride
Juliet Prowse
Esther Rantzen
Bertice Reading
Lyn Redgrave
Christopher Reeve
Debbie Reynolds
Gary Rhodes
Wendy Richards
Angela Rippon
Ginger Rogers
Anton Rodgers
Patricia Routledge
Jane Russell
Dr Ruth
Sir Sydney Samuelson
Telly Savalas
Sir Jimmy Savile
Prunella Scales
George C Scott
Sir Harry Secombe
Peter Sellers
Jack Smethurst
Delia Smith

Jon Snow
Robert Stack
Terence Stamp
Tommy Steele
Sharon Stone
Meryl Streep
Jimmy Tarbuck
Bill Tarmey
Chris Tarrant
Gillian Taylforth
Elizabeth Taylor
James Taylor
Shaw Taylor
Christopher Timothy
Anthony Worral
Thompsonhhfgh
John Travolta
Twiggy
Liv Ullman
Sir Peter Ustinov
Bill Waddington
Robert Wagner
Barbara Windsor
Alan Whicker
Richard Whitley
Desmond Wilcox
Simon Williams
Ernie Wise
Natalie Wood
Helen Worth
Timothy West
Michael York

Sports Personalities Who Have Travelled:

Eric Bristow
Frank Bruno
Sir Matt Busby
Jack Charlton
Sir Colin Cowdry
Brian Close
Kenny Dalglish
Steve Davis
Keith Deller
Alan Hansen
Stephen Hendry
Denis Law
Cliff Lazarenko
David Platt
Tessa Sanderson
Nobby Stiles
Daley Thompson
Murray Walker

Spacemen Who Have Travelled:

Buzz Aldrin

Titanic Survivors Who Have Travelled:

Millvina Dean

Explorers Who Have Travelled

Colonel John Blashford-Snell
Sir Chris Bonington
Jean-Michel Cousteau
John Harrison
Sir Wally Herbert
Brian Jones
Dr Kathryn L Sullivan
Stephen Venables

Cultural Authorities Who Have Travelled:

Julia Child
Giancarlo Impiglia
Leroy Neiman

Philanthropists Who Have Travelled:

J.Paul Getty Jnr

Queen Mary 2
Queen Victor

Three Queens Rendezvous

For the first and last time in their history, Cunard Line's Three Queens met together in their home port of Southampton in April, 2008.

Queen Mary 2 and Queen Victoria were in port together for a few hours between voyages. Queen Elizabeth 2 was undergoing a short refit and refurbishment following her last world cruise and before the start of her final season in service for Cunard Line.

To mark the historic occasion, special arrangements were made for the departure of QM2 on the afternoon of April, 22.

The flagship of the Cunard fleet was at her normal berth alongside the Queen Elizabeth II Terminal. Queen Victoria was using Southampton's City Cruise Terminal and QE2 was moored alongside another adjacent quay in the busy port.

Detailed planning between Cunard Line, the Masters of the three liners, and the port authorities allowed for QM2 to leave her berth and, instead of heading out towards the Isle of Wight and the English Channel, the mighty transatlantic liner headed up Southampton Water towards her sisters.

A huge flotilla of small craft crowded the Queen as she made her way towards the historic rendezvous.

Earlier in the year the three sisters had met for the first time in New York but heavy rain and poor visibility blighted the spectacle played out at night in front of the Statue of Liberty.

On a beautiful spring afternoon in Southampton, the sun shone on the majestic parade and the tens of thousands of spectators filling the city's waterfront Mayflower Park and other vantage points.

Pleasure craft had been fully booked since the date had been announced, and light aircraft and helicopters buzzed overhead.

A little after 5.30pm QM2, bound for New York, let go her ropes and made slow, majestic progress towards her smaller sisters.

3 Queens in Southampton

QUEEN MARY 2 PASSES QE2 (LEFT)
WITH QUEEN VICTORIA AHEAD

As QM2 reached Queen Victoria, the first of the afternoon's prolonged whistle blasts between the Cunarders began.

Then it was the turn of the Old Girl to acknowledge the arrival of her big sister alongside and the presence of her younger sister elsewhere in the port.

QE2's distinctive booming whistle was given a long blast as QM2 sailed by. Members of QE2's crew lined her open decks and the starboard bridge wing to wave at their colleagues and guests on board QM2.

With astonishing manoeuvrability, QM2 turned in her own length to position herself for another spectacular sail past her two sisters.

More whistle blowing between the ships followed – this time punctuated by shorter, shrill blasts from the numerous yachts, motor launches, leisure craft, media boats and harbour launches joining the occasion.

As QM2 left her sister behind to start her six-day transatlantic crossing, Queen Victoria edged way from her berth, bound for the Canaries, blasting one final salute to QE2 - the only Cunard Queen left at home after an historic day in Southampton.

FALKLANDS DUTY

WAR SERVICE IN THE SOUTH ATLANTIC DURING THE SPRING AND EARLY SUMMER OF 1982 ENSURED ANOTHER HISTORIC CHAPTER IN THE LIFE OF THE MOST FAMOUS OCEAN LINER IN THE WORLD.

Her conversion from luxurious liner to troop carrier, helicopter base and communications link took just eight days and nights.

After Margaret Thatcher's government announced that a Task Force was to be assembled to sail to the South Atlantic in support of British dependants on the Falkland Islands, Britain's merchant fleet was called upon to provide extensive support, expertise and tonnage.

The decision to designate QE2 as Ship Taken up from Trade (STUFT) raised some eyebrows; she was, after all, the flagship of the British merchant fleet. Some expressed the view that her very presence, in what was to become a war zone, not to mention her heritage and status as a British icon, would make her a prime target for Argentine air and sea forces.

Regardless of many misgivings, Cunard Line was keen to be seen to be doing its bit for what was to become a full-blown war effort. The conversion work was complex.

Before it could even begin, the first task of an army of Cunard officers and crew, who had volunteered to stay onboard for this cruise with a difference, was to remove and protect as much of the ship's priceless art and décor as possible.

The packing was complete by the time QE2 left Southampton on the afternoon of May 12.

Some 3,000 members of the Fifth Infantry Brigade were settling in to their new surroundings. Sea King helicopters joined as the ship headed down the Solent and the 8,000 mile voyage towards whatever lay ahead in the South Atlantic was underway.

After stops at Sierrra Leone and Ascension Island, QE2 commenced the final leg of her journey towards the war zone. News reached those on board that the requisitioned merchant container vessel Atlantic Conveyor had been lost following an air strike by Argentine forces.

By May 26, QE2 was close enough to the war zone that she started to weave, rather than maintain a straight course.

The ship's radar had been turned off and full blackout implemented - both orders made to lessen the risk of detection by enemy forces.

Without radar to assist navigation and with thick mist and fog forming, icebergs became a serious threat.

After consultation with military commanders QE2's captain, Peter Jackson, reactivated the ship's radar. In the hours that followed, more than 100 icebergs, large enough to be picked up by radar, appeared on the ship's screen.

After the ice threat passed, plans were made for QE2 to rendezvous with other naval vessels to commence the transfer of troops.

On the evening of May 27, QE2 dropped anchor in Cumberland Bay, South Georgia, about a mile from the former whaling station which weeks earlier had witnessed the start of the conflict.

Troops and equipment were transferred to a variety of vessels ready for the fight to regain the islands which lay 200 miles to the east.

Survivors from three sunken Royal Navy ships, HMS Ardent, HMS Antelope and HMS Coventry were taken on board QE2. Finally, on June 3, orders were received for QE2 to start her long journey home with the survivors still on board.

By June 11, QE2 was back in more familiar waters off the Isle of Wight.

A tumultuous welcome awaited with HM The Queen and HM The Queen Mother aboard the Royal Yacht Britannia to lead official recognition of Cunard Line's latest contribution to a war effort.

A message from the Queen mother was flashed to QE2.

It read: 'I am pleased to welcome you back as QE2 returns to home waters after your tour of duty in the South Atlantic. The exploits of your own ship's company and the deeds of valor of those who served in Antelope, Coventry and Ardent, have been acclaimed throughout the land and I am proud to add my personal tribute.'

Captain Jackson replied with the words:

"Please convey to Her Majesty Queen Elizabeth our thanks for her kind message.

Cunard's Queen Elizabeth 2 is proud to have been of service to Her Majesty's forces."

The two messages have been engraved in silver and can be seen on board.

QE2 was home after a mission which took her almost 15,000 miles in just under 30 days. After refitting she returned to transatlantic duty departing Southampton on August 15.

QE2 RECEIVED A ROUSING WELCOME BACK TO THE UK AFTER WAR DUTY

QUEEN OF THE NORTH ATLANTIC

QE2 WAS BUILT FOR THE NORTH ATLANTIC – AND IT'S JUST AS WELL!

When the Liner lets go her ropes and leaves Southampton for the last time on November 11th, she will have made the crossing between Europe and North America an astonishing 806 times.

In July 1990, as the ship prepared to lead Cunard Line's 150th anniversary celebrations with a voyage round the British Isles, QE2 claimed a record for crossing the North Atlantic at an average speed of 30.36 knots.

That's around 35 mph in landlubber's money. Think about the sheer power required to drive a ship the size of QE2 through an ocean the size of the Atlantic at that average speed for four days and nights.

For that record run, under the command of Captain Robin Woodall the mighty liner left New York on time and in good weather, and, crucially, with good weather forecast for the crossing.

Precisely four days later she passed Bishop Rock light – the navigation point marking the end of the crossing.

"It was quick," admits Captain Woodall.

Quick indeed when you consider the journey has routinely been scheduled to take six days and nights.

Crossing the Atlantic with Cunard is one of life's great journeys. And on board the legendary QE2, crossings became the stuff of legends.

a Westbound passage from Southampton the ship has usually left her berth at the city's QEII Terminal by teatime on the day of departure.

By the time guests have settled in to their staterooms and first timers have started to familiarise themselves with their new surroundings – the ship has passed the Isle of Wight and passed into the English Channel bound for the Western Approaches.

A pre-dinner drink in the Chart Room, to the accompaniment of a harpist or pianist, marks a highlight of the first evening on board.

When passengers finally retire to their beds, QE2 is well on her way down the Channel and by dawn the next morning the vast open expanse of the North Atlantic beyond the Fastnet Rock beckons.

Fastnet Lighthouse is known as The Teardrop of Ireland, the last sight of Ireland for emigrants, or latter day travellers, sailing to America.

The rock itself is four and a half miles southwest of Cape Clear and southwest of Mizen Head.

Passing by on QE2 westbound for New York is a moving and memorable experience.

After this, its open sea all the way to Nantucket Island, 25 miles south of Cape Cod, south east Massachusetts.

It's possible to reach this point on a QE2 crossing without seeing a single other vessel during the 3,000 mile journey.

First such sightings are likely to be fishing boats. In these waters, QE2 often exchanged signals with another great icon of Transatlantic Travel – Concorde.

With the liner a matter of hours away from New York, the evening British Airways departure from John F Kennedy Airport for London could sometimes be heard breaking the sound barrier above QE2 as its pilot took his guests on their supersonic way across the pond.

Such were the timings on these occasions that QE2 guests hearing the supersonic bang on open decks at tea time, would likely be enjoying their final night's dinner on board by the time Concorde touched the tarmac at Heathrow. A certain case of more pace than grace!

After such an epic but often solitary journey ñ one completed by an estimated 34 million people between 1820 and 1920 – arrival in New York by dawn the next morning can be both exciting and bewildering.

To pass under the Verrazano Narrows Bridge linking Staten Island and Brooklyn sends a tingle down the spine. Soon after, to view Liberty and Ellis Island, and the unmistakable tip of the Manhattan skyline underlines the experience of the whole journey.

Cunard continues these legendary transatlantic crossings on board QE2's sister Queen Mary 2 and they remain a journey of a lifetime – in fair weather or foul.

Transatlantic voyages are not always blessed with good weather. Five years after Captain Woodall's record breaking run, QE2 had left Southampton bound for New York when the remnants of Hurricane Luis, which had wrought havoc in the Caribbean, were plotted ahead of the liner.

After monitoring worsening conditions and forecasts the ship altered its course to avoid the worst of the weather. Although the ferocity of the storm was lessening, freak waves remained a threat and on 10th September 1995 at 0210 hrs a large wave was sighted right ahead of the bow.

When it eventually crashed over the foredeck the ship juddered. Despite the commotion caused by the rogue wave, many passenger slept serenely through the night. The first they knew of the adventure was when they received a Storm Certificate the next day!

And during her maiden crossing, Queen Mary 2 encountered a Force 10 storm described by one passenger as 'howling around the ship like a marine banshee'.

Perversely, the great Atlantic can be mirror-glass flat for the duration of a crossing.

In all weathers, Cunard Line has maintained its scheduled transatlantic service for an incredible 168 years.

NAUTICAL BUT NICE, MARITIME MEMENTOS

A UNIQUE QUALITY GIFT

CAPTURE THE MAGIC OF THIS YEAR'S HISTORIC VISIT OF THE ARK ROYAL TO LIVERPOOL WITH THIS UNIQUE COMMEMORATIVE 16" X 12" PRINT

Postage & packaging is included in the price for UK orders. You can see the full range of our Ark Royal photographs by logging on to www.merseyshop.com/buyaphoto

FOR SALE - GLORIOUS SIGNED PRINTS BY THE LEADING MARITIME ARTIST TED WALKER FROM £12.00 PLUS P&P £4.00

For other great titles, special offers and a full price list visit www.merseyshop.com or call: 0845 143 0001